When Mom Goes to Work

When Mom Goes to Work

by
Mary Beth Moster

MOODY PRESS
CHICAGO

© 1980, by
Mary Beth Moster

All Scripture quotations except those noted otherwise are from the *New American Standard Bible*, © 1960, 1962, 1963, 1968, 1971, 1972, 1973, 1975, and 1977 by The Lockman Foundation, and are used by permission.

Scripture quotations designated NIV are from *Holy Bible: New International Version*. Copyright © 1978 by the New York International Bible Society. Used by permission of Zondervan Bible Publishers.

The use of selected references from various versions of the Bible in this publication does not necessarily imply publisher endorsement of the versions in their entirety.

Library of Congress Cataloging in Publication Data

Moster, Mary Beth

When Mom Goes to Work.

Includes biographical references.
1. Mothers—Employment—United States. 2. Mothers—Employment. I. Title.
HD6055.2.U6M67   331.4'4'0973   80-19906
ISBN 0-8024-9442-0

Printed in the United States of America

Contents

*To Steve, my encourager, sounding board,
and the spiritual leader of our home,
and to Jeff, Debbie, and Angela,
whose hard work and cooperation
helped make this book possible*

Preface

If you are a woman trying to balance the demands of motherhood as well as those of a paying job—or if you are thinking about entering the work force—you need *help*. You need help in dealing with emotional stress and family conflict. You need help in managing your busy life.

This book is for the woman who is combining motherhood with a paying job. It's for the woman who works either because she wants to or because she must. It's for the woman who is not working yet but is considering it. It's for the woman who is working and wants to have a baby, and for the pregnant woman who is trying to decide if she should continue working after the baby is born. It's for the working woman with children in elementary school or high school. It's for the woman who wants to find out how other women are managing. It is really for anyone who wants a better understanding of what happens to the woman and her family when she goes to work. Though the book is primarily directed to women, it is also for men, especially the husband of the working woman. It will help him better understand both his wife and this complicated issue.

Many books have been published on the subject of working mothers, but this one is *unique*. It truly is the *working* solution because it is based on the eternal truth of God and His Word. You will find that God's principles can be applied to your daily life in a very practical way. How do I know these ideas work? Other women have found them to work, and they are working every day in my own life.

To all the men and women involved in the preparation of this book—I thank you so very much. Your willingness to share with me your truimphs and trials, your fears and frustrations, your dreams and dilemmas has made this book one that can help many.

Scores of women, mothers who are employed outside the home, participated in this effort. Many of those women are married. Some have supportive husbands; some do not. A number of them are in the throes of divorce proceedings, some are recently separated, and some are learning to live as single parents.

Those women are from all over the country and work in all kinds of occupations. Most are not in glamorous jobs; they are the women who live on your street, shop at your supermarket, or ride in your elevator. They might, in some ways, be you.

Though I talked with people from New York to California, some Indiana people were especially helpful. A warm thanks goes to Jim Hanks, regional vice-president of the State Farm Insurance Company's regional office in Lafayette, Indiana, and to Tom Miller, chairman of the board of the Indiana National Bank, for consenting to my interviewing a number of their employees.

I am also grateful to Pastor Charles E. Perry, Jr., Whitestown Baptist Church, Whitestown, Indiana, for his contributions.

To my sister Judy Timberman, her husband Fred, and their daughters Lisa and Becky, I just want to say, "Thank you." Also I thank Rosalie Alexander, Jo Ann Hunt, Sonja Jones, Kay Moster, Joyce Runyan, Sally Tanselle, and Cindy Zeigler.

A very special thanks goes to Shirley Hoke who spent many hours typing and retyping the manuscript. I appreciate her insight and encouragement as a working mother, one who has "been there."

Especially I want to thank Phil and Myrna White who graciously allowed me to share their story. Except for their names, and a few taken from printed material, no real names are used. The situations have been altered to protect the identities of the people involved, and some accounts are fictional. If a name used belongs to an actual person, it is a coincidence.

A Message...

From One Husband to Another

Most marriages begin with romantic optimism even though surrounded by the many problems of today's world. Our marriage was no exception. We were married and blessed with our first two children during the war-associated sixties. Upon my return from military service we, like many others, began to settle into the young-married civilian environment. For a while we both worked. Saving money was our main, maybe only, true goal.

Those days were typically full of 5:30 wake-ups, breakfasts seemingly in the middle of the night, dressing half-asleep children, and scurrying off to the babysitter (which changed frequently). I also remember concern about leaving our children with some babysitters we barely knew. I remember we wished we did not have to do it. But, we did it anyway. At that point we just plowed through each week without much of a system. Whether or not we both really had to work then is now "after the fact" for us. You may want to take inventory of your circumstances to see if it is really necessary for your wife to work while children are still at home. The most important influence on them is the two of you.

At this point let's assume that you both are working at jobs in addition to running the household. Congratulations are in order if you already have a *working system* to manage everything. Still, I am confident you will find some helpful ideas in this book. The book is directed to the wife, but for the ideas to work, you will have to be in one accord. Don't let anybody kid you—running a household is a big, busy operation. Without your leadership and discipline, the kids won't want to participate in all this organizing, planning, and doing. Don't worry; that's normal. Improper management can create ulcers and unhappiness both at home and at work. With a "partnership commitment," close family relationships can be built with both husband and wife working away from the home. It isn't easy, but it is possible.

Why is it important to be concerned about your wife's work and the household in addition to your job? It's simple. Very possibly the best years of your life, the years of unforgettable family memories, are your children's growing-up years at home together. Certain moments you just can't have with the grandchildren if you miss them with your own family. Harmony comes from becoming a true family unit. You may have heard the saying "A family that prays together stays together." I would like to expand that to say, "A family that works, plays, and prays together has the greatest possible opportunity to succeed in achieving the most and the best that can possibly be gleaned from this short time we have together."

That can only be accomplished in an atmosphere of genuine love. The kind of love I am speaking of is not the romantic love that first "sparked" your marriage; rather, it is the kind of love that comes only by maturing together through family work and play. It is cemented by the bond of a spiritual growth-relationship. It is vital that you come to understand about God, His plan for each of us, His message to each of us, and learn about life's day-to-day principles through His Word.

At one point in my life after those early civilian years, I had to decide what was really important to me. That was necessary so that meaningful relationships could continue to grow rather than stagnate. I invite you to seriously consider those things, too, at this point in your life. This message is brief. I encourage you to read the remainder of the book for details and additional important points you need to consider. Yesterday is gone, but you don't have to wait until tomorrow to begin living today abundantly full.

May God bless you and the future of your family together.

From one husband to another,

Steve Moster

Steve Moster

Chapter One

America's Superwoman

If you are a working mother, you are America's new Superwoman.

You do it *all.*

A perfume commercial says:

> I can bring home the bacon
> Fry it up in a pan.
> And never, never, never
> let you forget you're a man.
> Cause I'm a woman.*

Wow. It sounds great!

Your day must go something like this:

You leap out of bed at 4:00 A.M. and jump into your jogging shoes for a three-mile trek around the neighborhood. Before anybody is awake, you have breakfast prepared, lunch packed, and dinner in the Crock-Pot.

That *is* how it works, isn't it?

You sweep through the house, picking up and shining up, then wake the kids with a hug and hubby with a kiss.

Right?

Then you, in a very orderly fashion, see that the older children are dressed and ready for the day and that the baby is bathed and talcumed.

---

*Quoted from television advertisement for ENJOLI Fragrance by permission of Charles of the Ritz Group Ltd.

17

You whirl around a couple of times *voilà!*—perfect hair, flawless makeup, designer clothes.

A loving, grandmotherly woman stays with the children in your home, so with an air of serenity you leave for work, confident that your children are in competent hands.

And what has your husband been doing all that time? Why, looking at you with misty-eyed admiration, of course. You are *Superwoman,* remember.

On weekends you all work together to take care of the housework and laundry. It gives you such a feeling of "togetherness."

At work you are the marvel of the office. You work with the utmost efficiency and wisdom, climbing the career ladder of success and fulfillment. The paycheck, naturally, is what gives you a feeling of self-worth.

After work, you have a joyous reunion with the children. They are so secure and well adjusted that they are perpetually cheerful and cooperative; you in turn are relaxed and free from tension. You play a quick game with the children and help them a few minutes with their homework, remembering that it is the *quality* of time, not the quantity, that counts.

The evening meal is a time of lively, animated discussion. (Your husband finds you so much more *interesting* now.) And after the children have been tucked into bed, you and your husband enjoy the evening together, finding that even your love life has improved since you became Superwoman.

Oh.

You say that is not exactly what goes on at your house?

It could be that you believe 4:00 A.M. should be taken off the clock. Maybe you need to be given your coffee intravenously to regain consciousness in the mornings. And breakfast? Would you believe droopy eyelids and Froot Loops are the rule rather than the exception?

It is bedlam before breakfast, as the battle for the bathroom begins. You think, *Someday we've got to get a system around here.* But every day it's the early birds that get the hot water, and everyone else squawks.

You discover that the "grandmotherly woman who comes to your home" is, for the most part, a myth. Real grandmas might occasionally be available to stay with their grandchildren, but reality shows that Grandma usually lives halfway across the country or else she has found a job of her own. That means that it is necessary to haul the baby out to a sitter and hope the older kids do not kill each other during the two hours they are home alone after school.

There are problems at work, too. You were told that you could find fulfillment in a job. You found that, yes, certain aspects of it are satisfying. But mostly, it is just routine, even boring, *work.*

When you get home from work in the evenings, you find that you are too often frazzled from a rough day. So you scream at Jimmy for spilling his milk. When Scott talks back to you, you just let it pass because you are too tired to get into a hassle. When Susie asks if she can have a friend over to stay all night, you say no before even thinking about it. Then you let her whine and badger you into saying yes because you are just too exhausted to fight about it, and, anyway, you feel you should not have said no in the first place.

You see the children having problems as they grow older, and you get a severe case of "the guilts." You are told that it is just the "conditioning" that little girls get during childhood that makes you feel guilty, so you do not dare ask the questions: Is Scott getting that sarcastic mouth because I'm working? Would Jimmy have more self-confidence if I were with him more? Would Susie make better grades if I were home?

You have secret worries about your husband, too. He seems to think it's fine that you work, but why doesn't he participate more in the care of the children? Why doesn't he pitch in and help around the house?

When evening rolls around, you are exhausted. You have

done everything you used to do when you were home all day, plus you have worked at your job. You ask yourself, "This is liberation?"

You have been led to believe that it is not only possible but *easy* to be Superwoman. It is not.

Getting Everything Done can become an obsession. How do other women do it? Or do they? Is it possible? Will the family be able to survive? What about the children?

Many different factors must be considered when a mother is thinking about taking a job outside the home. Here are a few of them:

• The ages of the children. The younger the children, the more they need nurturing, parenting, and *time*. If the mother or father doesn't care for them on a day-to-day basis, who will?

• The demands of single parenthood. Single mothers who must work full time to financially support the family are under a double load.

• The demands of the husband's job and the wife's job. How stress-producing are those jobs? How time-demanding? How flexible? How well do they fit into the demands at home? Can anything be changed to make things run more smoothly?

• How committed are both the mother and father to providing a warm, nurturing atmosphere at home?

• What can be done to insure that the limited time together will benefit the family? Is there such a thing as "quality" time? Of course there is, but quality time *takes* time. Children can't be plugged in when convenient, and children's needs can't be neatly checked off on a "Things to Do" list.

• How does your husband view your working? Does he feel threatened by it? Can you talk about it without one or both of you becoming upset?

• Is he willing to become more involved in child care and housework? Does he see those responsibilities as "woman's work"? Will he resent it, or will he enjoy it? Can you talk about it?

• Will your job conflict with your husband's job? What would happen if either of you was offered a transfer to another city?

Full-Time Homemaker "Obsolete"?

For millions of women, going to work already is or soon may be an economic necessity. With inflation devouring the family's budget at a terrifying rate, husbands and wives across this country and in all the Western world are facing the harsh reality that one income often is simply not enough.

The situation is so pressing that Caroline Bird, author of *The Two-Paycheck Marriage*, says that the full-time homemaker is now "obsolete" simply because of economic pressures.[1]

It is not really a new thing for women to work, because throughout history many women have been forced economically to do so. But it is something new to see millions of middle-class women leave their comfortable suburban homes and enter what they call the "real world."

For the first time in any society, a wife's career might be considered as important as her husband's, leading to a phenomenon called "dual careerism." The dual-career revolution is causing stress in families and dilemmas for corporations forced to think about "spouse accommodation."

At the beginning of the 1980s, well over 40 million American women were working for pay. That is about 50 percent of the civilian labor force. *U.S. News and World Report* says, "Women are swelling the work force at a rate of almost two million every year—a phenomenon that is beginning to transform everyday life in the United States."[2]

In the same article, Eli Ginzberg, head of the National Commission for Manpower Policy, says, "It changes the relationship of men to women: it changes the relationship of mothers to children. And the future of the suburbs may also be in doubt."[3]

A new study by the Urban Institute suggests that by 1990,
three-fourths of all married women and two-thirds of all
mothers will hold jobs. And not only are more women working, they are working longer. On the average, women today
work 22.9 years as opposed to 12 years in 1940.

"Dick and Jane" Family Disappearing

The "Dick and Jane" family of the old first grade primer is
quickly disappearing. (Surely some of you remember: Father
goes to work, Dick and Jane play happily with dog Spot,
Mother is simply *there*.) The typical American family has
been redefined by the Federal Bureau of Labor Statistics to
include a mother as well as a father working outside the
home. In recent years a kind of reversal has taken place.
Working mothers used to be the ones to be criticized; now
full-time mothers find themselves repeatedly having to de-
fend their being "just housewives."

Christian wives and mothers are also working, and those
who do not have jobs outside the home are under the same
pressures as other women to do something "meaningful."

Recently a group of Christian couples were gathered for an
evening of fellowship. The husbands were introducing their
wives by telling the group what they did. Each man proudly
introduced his wife and told where she worked. Only *one* of
the women at that gathering did not have a job outside the
home. After an awkward silence, her husband said, "My
wife's a domestic engineer." The nervous laughter didn't help
much. *That* is pressure.

It is, perhaps, not surprising that half of all women of working age in this country are employed. It *is* startling to realize
that half of all mothers of school-age children work. An as-
tonishing 40 percent of women with preschool children work
away from home; that figure is extremely significant when we
realize that the number has tripled since 1950. Women with

children have been identified as the fastest-growing segment of the working population.

A number of books have been written on the subject of working mothers. The issue has been examined and reexamined psychologically, sociologically, historically, and hysterically. Experts have come out of their ivory towers, data clutched in hand, to state their conflicting opinions.

"Children of working mothers are going to grow up deprived of the most essential form of nurturing—mothering," some insist. "They will be hopelessly maladjusted."

"Children of working mothers are more independent, self-reliant, and capable than the children of mothers who stay at home," others counter.

"Women who work are destroying the role of husband as breadwinner. It's breaking down the very foundation of the family," some say.

"Marriages where both husband and wife work are stronger," others reply.

And on it goes.

So what is a mother to do? Whom can she believe?

Mothers need help in dealing with the emotional stress and conflict that working can cause. Where can they turn for answers?

The Bible is a Book of answers, having principles for living that are timeless and eternal. In that Book we can find practical solutions for today's problems.

Some people believe that the Bible is too ancient, too outdated to have relevance in today's world. Others believe that it is sexist and demeans women. What a joy to discover that the basic message of the Bible is one of *liberation* and *freedom*.

In spite of that fact, Christian mothers often have been given the impression that it is wrong to work and that any woman who takes a job outside the home is hurting her family. When she is forced to go to work to make ends meet, she is haunted by doubt and fear. When she wants to work because she truly enjoys her work, she is torn by conflict and guilt.

Many people might be convinced that the Christian viewpoint is briefly stated: "A woman's place is in the home."

That statement, though it is accepted as true by many persons, does not come from the Bible. "A woman's place is in the home" is a modern paraphrase of a remark made by the Greek dramatist Aeschylus: "Let women stay home and hold their peace." Later the thought was expressed by a German proverb: "The fish is happy in the water, the bird in the air, and the good woman at home." I repeat, that oft-quoted statement does not come from God's Word.

But what, if anything, does the Bible say about working mothers? Is there a Scriptural directive forbidding mothers to work?

The Bible tells us in Proverbs 31 about a woman who is both godly and virtuous. Her life is described in eloquent detail, and it is clear that she did work outside the home. She was given areas of financial responsibility. And that passage of Scripture was written, incidentally, when a woman was considered by society to be mere chattel, part of her husband's property. It is interesting to note that that "ideal woman" was confined by neither stereotype nor preconceived notions about a woman's "place."

She worked in real estate and agriculture: "She considers a field and buys it; from her earnings she plants a vineyard" (v. 16).

She was involved in the area of manufacturing, sales, and marketing; "She makes linen garments and sells them, and supplies belts to the tradesmen" (v. 24).

She also was an excellent home manager: "She looks well to the ways of her household, and does not eat the bread of idleness. Her children rise up and bless her; her husband also, and he praises her, saying 'Many daughters have done nobly but you excel them all' " (v. 27-29).

The Bible recognizes other women in the working situation. Aquila and his wife, Priscilla, were tentmakers who worked with the apostle Paul. Lydia was a successful woman in sales, and Deborah was a judge and military leader.

It is indeed possible to combine motherhood with a job. But in order for it to be a truly successful combination—one that will be good for the marriage, the family, and the mother—it must be done according to God's principles.

Notes

[1] From "Full-Time Homemaking Is Now 'Obsolete,' " a copyrighted interview in *U.S. News & World Report*, 9 July 1979, p. 47.

[2] From "Working Women: Joys and Sorrows," a copyrighted article in *U.S. News & World Report*, 15 January 1979, p. 64.

[3] Ibid.

Chapter Two

The Feminine Mistake?

Betty Friedan struck a nerve in 1963 with *The Feminine Mystique.*

She described vividly and in great detail the feelings of loneliness and frustration felt by millions of American women.

She analyzed the women's magazines of the times and found "The Happy Housewife Heroine" image to be the total emphasis of those magazines during the 1950s and early 1960s. Magazine editors, she reported, were convinced that women were not interested in ideas, or issues, or anything other than home, husband, and children. Women were pictured as housewives whose greatest joy was centered in the family, whose most profound fulfillment rested in the mothering role.

Friedan observed that under that veneer of "happiness" was a very discontented woman, a woman who would lie awake at night sobbing to herself, *Is this all there is?*

She investigated the world of advertising and was horrified to find marketing specialists, especially television advertisers, totally dedicated to keeping women at home, buying their products. They were determined to see to it that women found their fulfillment in eliminating static cling and ring-around-the-collar.

The Feminine Mystique caused a shock wave felt in homes across America and around the world. Middle-class women especially were struck by Friedan's message. Women rallied around her, and the modern women's liberation movement was born. The reason that book had such an impact is that much of what Friedan said was true.

Women had been told that their fulfillment in life could be found in mothering, and *they were not fulfilled.* Friedan identified "the problem that had no name," and millions, *millions* of women started marching to the beat of her drum.

It was true that women were not fulfilled by motherhood alone. Empty hearts were *yearning* to find that elusive fulfillment.

Why was motherhood in itself unable to satisfy a searching heart?

A Fairy Tale

The American woman had believed a fairy tale. Prince Charming would come along, and the two of them would live happily ever after. Through *him* she would find peace and serenity in her heart. Through her children she could find fulfillment.

It was not true.

She could deeply love her husband and children, but she had an emptiness in her heart that even they could not fill. Something was missing—but what?

Prince Charming was a human being with his own problems. The children were demanding and often irritating. She did not find the "bundle of joy" to be much fun when crying, whining, or stomping through mud puddles.

Mrs. Prince Charming did not know that her husband was also searching for the same elusive happiness. She did not know that he, too, felt a void in his life. His silent moods, outbursts of anger, and excessive social drinking should have told her something.

All she knew was that *she* was the one at home all day with babies, diapers, and runny noses. She thought about her husband out there in the "real world," and she resented being tied down by children and the baby-factory image.

The Feminine Mistake

Betty Friedan did an excellent job of analyzing and assessing the problem. But the solution she offered was inadequate. She saw men out there, working in the areas of business, medicine, science, and government. They *seemed* free. Surely they had the answer.

That was it! A job!

Friedan said it, and millions believed it: *"The only way for a woman, as for a man, to find herself, to know herself as a person, is by creative work of her own"* (emphasis mine).[1]

A job outside the home seemed to be the answer to the unhappy housewife's feelings of frustration. But when she entered the job market, she found millions of other women already there, working diligently but no more "fulfilled" than the housewife at home. Many women, as a matter of fact, could not understand what all the fuss was about. They, it seemed, had *always* worked.

If ordinary jobs were not fulfilling, then the problem must be that what women needed were more important jobs, more power, more money.

To a certain extent, women had been denied educational and career opportunities, and it was imperative to face the fact that women had been locked into jobs that paid poorly and offered little or no hope of advancement. Reforms were needed in those areas.

But sadly, one fairy tale replaced another. Instead of Prince Charming's showing the way to true happiness and fulfillment, now career success would be the answer to all problems. Without career success, a woman's talents would be wasted; she would be a failure. Career success would make her secure; it would transform her into the independent, confident woman she had always hoped to be. If she could only have career success, she would be fulfilled.

The only problem was: it didn't work. Women soon discovered what men in the business world had known all along but were afraid to admit: success on the job does not guarantee happiness.

It was frustrating. If living happily ever after with Prince Charming was not the answer, and having babies was not truly fulfilling, and career success could not satisfy the deepest longings of a person's heart—then *what?*

Real Fulfillment in a Real World

Sally Benson is a woman who graduated from college in the late 1950s. She married Alan, had four children, and was involved in mothering when the modern women's movement began surfacing.

"I could really identify with the feminists," says Sally, "because I was living out in the suburbs in PTA, Cub Scouts, and chicken pox. I had graduated with a business major, and here I was cleaning up orange juice from the kitchen floor. Ugh.

"I went to some consciousness-raising group meetings, and it was there that I learned about the terrible plight of women, how they had been discriminated against, how they had been abused for centuries and put down by men.

"When I got home after a meeting, I was furious with my husband (who had, incidentally, stayed home with the kids so I could go). I would be lying next to him in bed at night and feel so *cold* toward him. After all, he was a *man*, and just look at what men had done to women over the years."

Sally became more and more involved in the women's movement. She soon believed she needed to "find herself" through "creative work of her own."

Sally says, "I began to see that all those years I had had no identity of my own. I was always Alan's wife or Todd's mother. But who was I?"

So Sally went to work.

"I really didn't have much trouble finding a job. I went to work in the local telephone company in the business office. I didn't have any secretarial background, but it didn't seem to matter because I had a degree. At that point the telephone company was making a real effort, because of government pressure, not only to hire women but to move them into management positions.

"So it wasn't long before I was really going places career-wise. And I was loving it.

"But things at home were falling apart. Jamey, the baby, was not adjusting well at the sitter's house. I had a nagging fear that he was being parked in front of the television set all day. Also the sitter's little boy was bratty, and I worried about Jamey's picking up his bad habits.

"The older kids were in school most of the day, so that part should have been great. But they got home at 3:30 and stayed without an adult until 6:00 P.M. Some evenings I'd get home and the place would be in shambles. Other kids would be here, kids whose mothers were at work. They were drinking up our Cokes and leaving rings on our furniture. Schoolbooks and coats and other debris were deposited on top of the mess we had left in the morning. It was awful."

Alan, her husband, withdrew into a shell. He was torn between the way he really felt (not wanting her to work) and the way he thought he should feel (not wanting to stand in her way).

He began "working late" because he could not stand the confusion at home. He was having problems with his job, but Sally was always so swamped or preoccupied with her career that she did not listen when he tried to talk about it.

"I was usually upset with him anyway," she says, "because he refused to help me with anything around the house.

He'd said, "Go ahead. Get a job if you want to. But just because you're taking on more, don't expect me to take on more with you.'

"So he refused to lift a finger around the house. I'll admit it was a shock to him. I'd always waited on him hand and foot, then suddenly I refused to wait on him anymore. 'Get it yourself' became my standard reply.

"There were plenty of people who sympathized with me. At work many of the other women were having the same problem. Oh, there were a few who bragged about how wonderful and supportive their husbands were, but most of us had plenty to talk about in our gripe sessions over lunch.

"Then one day the roof caved in. Alan came in one night very late and woke me up. His face had no expression. He only said two words. 'I'm leaving.' I stared in amazement as he packed his bags. His eyes were cold, set.

"Later I found that he had been having an affair for several weeks with one of the women at his firm.

"I don't know how you are supposed to feel at a time like that, but I was furious. How could he do that to me after I had given him all those years and all those children?

"I tried to throw myself into my work. It was the only area where I felt halfway successful. So I worked hard and long.

"One day a friend at work, Sarah, invited me to have lunch with her at a ladies' Bible study. I didn't really know her very well. She never attended our lunchtime gripe sessions. The first time she invited me, I said, 'No, thanks!' I thought to myself, *Bible study—are you kidding me? I thought that went out with the horse and buggy!* And anyway, Alan and I had been through the whole bit of going to church. We had gone to church because it was what 'nice' people did, but frankly, I couldn't see much point in it. I got a little sick of all those people trying to convince each other about how good they were. No, Sarah could have her Bible study, thanks. I had tried religion, and it didn't work.

"But Sarah didn't give up on me. She kept asking me to go with her, so finally I consented. I was so surprised at the women there. Somehow I had visions of frowning women in long black dresses, with hair pulled back into severe and unattractive buns. These women were all smiling and happy. They greeted me warmly. Many of them were other businesswomen like myself.

"The leader of the study was a warm and attractive woman in her early forties. She got right into the Bible study because so many of us were on our lunch breaks. I don't remember much about the lesson, except she talked a lot about Jesus Christ. I felt uncomfortable, because the only time I heard that name was when someone was swearing. It seemed strange to hear her talking about Jesus Christ as though He was her friend.

"I kept going to the study with Sarah. Soon I began to realize that the Bible is a very special Book. I had always thought that only ignorant, uneducated people believed the Bible, but here was a room full of very sharp women. Many of them believed the Bible to be totally true and relevant for today. I thought that maybe there might be some hope in it for me.

"One day I went to the study, and I heard something I had never heard before—at least I hadn't understood it before. And that was that God loves me, that He cares about me and my life. I always thought that God was way out there, someplace. The universe is so huge. Was it possible that a God powerful enough to create all the stars and planets and solar systems could care about me?

"Then I found out why I felt so far away from God, like there was a barrier between us. That barrier was sin. I had no trouble remembering many of the wrong things I had done. I also felt like such a failure, especially as far as my family was concerned. I knew that many of my problems were the result of my own selfishness.

"The most amazing thing I heard was that God became a man, Jesus Christ, and that when He died on the cross, He was paying the penalty for my sin. He made it possible for me to have a personal relationship with God, if only I would accept Him as my Lord and Savior. It seemed so simple, but it made more sense to me than anything I'd heard in such a long time. So right there at the study I just invited Jesus Christ to come into my life, to forgive me for the way I'd messed up my life, and to change me into the kind of woman He had designed me to be.

"I really didn't feel much different that day. And the next day I wondered if I had just been silly and naive. I mean, really, what made me think God cared that much for me? But Sarah stayed close to me, and she patiently answered all of my many, many questions. She showed me in the Bible how my sins were as scarlet, but now they were as white as snow (Isaiah 1:18). She showed me how God had removed them as far as the east is from the west (Psalm 103:12). She showed me that God had given me a brand new life (1 Corinthians 5:17).

"And what a change it has made in me. I didn't really change in a sudden, dramatic way. But it's been about a year now since I invited Jesus to come into my life, and I know I'm a different person. I'm not perfect—not by a long shot. But I know that He is changing me. With Jesus Christ in charge of my life, my family situation is getting so much better. I'm being more of a mother to the children. I'm still working, but I'm not being tossed about by all the different philosophies I hear. Now I have something with which to evaluate those philosophies.

"One more thing I must tell you. At first I thought that because I had truly become a Christian that God would bring Alan back to me. It hasn't happened. He doesn't understand what has happened to me. But at least we can talk occasionally. And I have accepted the fact that Alan may not come back, ever. But I'm just trusting God for each day. The children and I have found a church that teaches the Bible and has a wonderful ministry to single adults. I thank God for the friends and fellowship I have there.

"God has granted me a peace of heart and peace of mind that is hard for me to describe. To realize that He is *God* and that He *loves* me is almost beyond comprehension. But what a difference it makes to know that.

"I am still working and doing very well in my job. I no longer feel that I'm doing this work to show everyone how liberated I am. Because now I am truly free. 'If therefore the Son shall make you free, you shall be free indeed' (John 8:36). I just thank God for showing me the way to real liberation and real fulfillment."

Notes

[1] Betty Friedan, *The Feminine Mystique* (New York: Norton, 1963), p. 344.

Chapter Three

Who Cares for the Children?

Marie Johnson remembers it as the most terrible day of her life. She got up after a night of turning and tossing. A dull, horrible ache throbbed somewhere deep inside. She made her way into the shower and turned it on full force.

"With the shower on," she says quietly, "I let myself scream—and moan—and cry. My baby was only two months old, and I was leaving her to go to work."

Her husband had made the decision for her. "We can't get the bills paid unless you work," he had said bluntly.

So, with an aching heart and overwhelming guilt feelings, she took the baby to the sitter.

"The people I met at work weren't all that much help," she says. "A lot of them seemed *glad* to get away from their kids—others said, 'Oh, yeah, I used to feel that way. Don't worry, you'll get over it.'

"Well, I didn't get over it. I adjusted, of course, but it still broke my heart that I missed seeing her first steps, hearing her first words. When she was tall enough to stand at the sitter's door as I left, she would sometimes cry and scream, 'Mommy, Mommy!' through the screen. There were times when I wondered if I could bear it.

"Later, my husband got a promotion. By this time he was making good money—between us we were making $40,000 a year. In 1978 that was good money. You'd think we would've had enough to pay our bills. But, you know, my working didn't solve our financial problems at all. We still couldn't seem to get our bills paid. I began to really resent my husband for being such a poor money manager. I began to see that if he had not kept buying new cars, and ski equipment, and all kinds of things we didn't really need, I would have been able to have stayed home with my baby. I don't know if it hurt *her* to be raised by the sitter. I'm sure it hurt *me*. I have a sense of loss that I may never get over."

Working Mother's Anxiety

The term *working mother* can refer to a woman with an outside job and a child or children in any stage of growing up, whether babies, toddlers, elementary school children, or high schoolers. The problems encountered during each stage of the child's life are different.

A working mother with a baby or very small child, however, is bound to be the one to have more conflicts and feelings of anxiety when she goes to work. Who will care for her baby?

The importance of what happens during that first five years has been well documented. Many child-development experts believe that most of the basic life-patterns and personality traits are set during early childhood. Much attention recently has been given to the phenomenon of "mother bonding," in which the child and mother form that close, intimate relationship that will be important to the child throughout his lifetime.

Other experts have rejected many of those basic ideas, saying it does not matter who takes care of the child as long as the person is kind and loving and provides an environment of nurturing.

Mothers who work are frankly confused by all the conflicting "expert" opinion. The trend today is to dismiss the mother's fears as slightly irrational and point to success stories of women who have left their babies with no ill effects.

Women's magazines seem to be especially fond of featuring "supermoms." One woman might be a nuclear physicist who has the baby brought to the lab for breastfeeding during coffee breaks. Or they tell about the woman pediatrician who manages her work and seven children with ease. Another woman might be a manufacturing executive changing a diaper during a sales conference. Another story might be of a television reporter who rushes off to cover a bank robbery with her two-year-old child in her arms.

For every woman who can take her baby with her to work and have him take a nap in a file drawer while she makes executive decisions, there are untold millions of women who have to leave their babies in the care of someone else.

Should You Work?

Some new mothers have no choice about working. Somebody has to provide the food, shelter, and clothing, and she is it. For those women, there will be help later in the chapter concerning finding good care for your child.

Mothers who do have a choice: Please think carefully. Weigh all aspects of this decision.

Those early months and years of your baby's life are critical to your child's growth and development. The physical aspects of nurturing—the food, the cleanliness, the opportunity to explore and learn—are all important. At least as important as the physical are the emotional aspects of nurturing. Studies have shown that infants who are deprived of love and affection just wither up and die. It is now known that half of a child's capacity to learn is developed by four years of age; 80 percent of the intellectual capacity is set by the time the child is eight.[1] The child's value system is also set very early.

God designed mothers to be the primary nurturers of the very young. It is the mother who produces the life-sustaining milk, and her arms don't hang straight down like a man's. Her arm has a natural bend at the elbow, providing the perfect cradle for a baby.[2]

It is not an easy job to take care of babies. Few jobs outside the home are as demanding and as generally unappreciated. But it is worth it.

If the mother cannot take care of the baby, can the father? God gives a child two parents and expects them both to be involved in the care of that little one.

Nobody in the world loves this child in the same way the two of you do. Nobody is as sensitive to his or her needs.

I will plead with you for a moment. Don't put your baby in someone else's care for the majority of the day simply to acquire a material thing that will wear out. Don't do it for new carpeting or new furniture. Long after that carpeting has worn out, your son or daughter will be living out the values taught in the early years and will probably be passing them along to future generations.

Some women go back to work right away to protect their jobs. Though many companies now have good maternity plans, few can guarantee that women can move back into the same job unless they go back within a very short time. Many women also want to return to work quickly to show that they are, indeed, fully committed to their work. Some very career-oriented women are surprised at the emotional tug-of-war that they experience when they go back to work.

It is a decision that you and your husband need to make *prayerfully*.

Choosing a Caretaker

Next to you and your husband, the adults most important in your child's life are the grandparents. Few children have the blessing anymore of really getting to know all four grand-parents, but the grandparents should be the first people considered if you must find someone else to care for the baby.

When considering a grandparent, think about these things:

• Do *you* have a good relationship with that person? Can you work together well and not find fault with each other? It is trickier with a relative than with someone not so close.

As I talked with mothers, I found several who were having the grandparents care for the children. Though some mothers were enthusiastic about how well it worked out for her mother or her husband's mother to babysit, other women said it just did not work on a long-term basis.

"My mother took over too completely," says one mother of a preschool child. "She became the authority on my daughter, and I resented it. Even though I was working, I still wanted to be my child's mother. I found a very kind woman to take care of her, and to me it was worth the extra money. I needed a more businesslike arrangement for her care, one that was not emotionally charged, one where I could give instructions. It's worked out fine, and I still have my mother as a backup when the sitter is sick or something. She enjoys it a lot more that way, too."

• Is the grandparent in good health?

• Does the grandparent *want* this responsibility? Many times grandparents are very glad when their children are grown, and raising another child is not what they had in mind as a way to enjoy the sunset years.

• Does the grandparent share your Christian beliefs and values? If not, you should find someone who does.

Who Else?

If the grandparents are not a possibility, then you might have someone else in the extended family who would be interested. A neighbor might be an even more workable possibility. If at all possible, find someone you know and trust.

Remember that a baby can't tell you if something bad is happening with the sitter, so be sure that your sitter is someone who is loving, patient, and kind.

A little child is like a sponge, sopping up everything that he hears, sees, and touches. He does not, cannot, discriminate between the bad and the good. I remember how horrified I was one time in a grocery store to hear a sweet little two-year-old girl chattering away, spouting profanities right and left. Her mother was embarrassed, mumbling something about her "picking it up" at the sitter's.

The child will "pick up" language, attitudes, habits, and values from whomever cares for him or her.

The Great Divide

In terms of group *day care*, there is usually a division of babies into two groups: those who are potty-trained and those who are not. At the time of this writing, the vast majority of day care for babies is for those who are out of diapers. As a general rule, however, infants need one-on-one attention from a caring adult, anyway.

As more women go to work, there will, no doubt, be more group programs open for infants, and some of those will be very good. For example, a few companies are even operating child-care centers at the site for their employees. At Photo Corporation of America, in North Carolina, a successful child-care center has been operating for seven years. At that center even nursing mothers are welcome to leave their babies. When it is feeding time, Mom is called, and she can drop her work to go and nurse the baby.[3]

That kind of situation is unusual. Day-care centers for the most part are not available for tiny babies, and few women in private homes will care for them either.

If you believe that hiring an individual is your best solution, try to make the decision very carefully and thoughtfully. One of the most important things is to find someone who is dependable. A baby or small child needs the safety and security of *one special person*. Hopping around from sitter to sitter does not provide that kind of stability. The mother of a year-old baby told me that she is on her fourth sitter since going back to work when the child was two months old. That situation is a hassle for her and is confusing for the baby. However if you find that the sitter you have hired is not working out, you must make other arrangements.

Another mother says that she found good sitters by placing an advertisement in the newspaper. "That way," she says, "*you* are in control. They come to you, and you are interviewing them—instead of the other way around. You can be in charge, and that helps."

Another place to find wonderful sitters is through the local church. Many times an older woman who is experienced working in the church nursery and loves children would be just the person you have been seeking.

Do you live near a college or university campus? Some times college students need extra income and are good with children if you can work out scheduling problems. Be sure to check references on any sitter you do not know personally.

The most popular form of day care (about 40 percent) is taking the child to a nonrelative's home where the child will be watched along with two or three other children. Interestingly enough, in many states that kind of day care is illegal without a license. In practice, licensed day care is rare. The day-care mothers in Milford, Illinois, for example, became so incensed over the licensing issue that they went underground, making finding a sitter in Milford "a little like getting into a speakeasy during Prohibition days. You have to have the right connections. Child-care has become a black-market operation."[4]

Group day care is growing. In the 1980s day care centers will pop up like fast-food restaurants, mainly because the women who used to take care of children in their homes for a little extra money are now going out themselves to get jobs in the business world.

Attitude Most Important

"The problem with day-care regulations," says one mother

of two toddlers, "is that they can define the physical facility, but there's not much way you can legislate *attitude*. And as far as I'm concerned, it's the attitude of the person who's caring for my child that makes the most difference to me. I looked over several day-care centers before I made a decision. I found that sometimes the owners and administrators were very good people, but the people they employed were just terrible. A woman who worked at one day-care center I checked out was just awful. She was so hateful and rude, I wouldn't have wanted her to take care of my *dog*."

Calico Cottage

An example of excellent day care is in the small town where I live. Pat Shoemaker is a certified teacher who loves children and takes a personal interest in each of the children in her care at Calico Cottage. She has a small group of children, so is qualified as a "day-care home" rather than a "day-care center."

She even takes home movies of the children, and one of their greatest delights is watching themselves on the screen.

One mother described her feelings this way: "Pat would make a wonderful mother for Ashley. She is very easy-going, yet keeps everything well-organized and predictable. It's a pleasure to go to work, knowing my child is in such capable hands."

Good day care *is* available. Just keep looking until you find it.

Some Pointers

Here are some tips from mothers who have traveled the day-care route.

For babies:

• How many children are being cared for, and how old are they? What is the ratio between children and adults? The younger the children, the fewer one adult can handle. One or two babies per adult is about all that anyone can adequately care for. You will have to evaluate the situation but be *on guard* for too many children. It is hard to handle infants, and it gets harder as they start crawling and exploring. Don't put an infant in a situation where there are more than one or two other children.

• Find out your sitter's attitude toward potty-training. How did she train her own kids? Does it make her nervous? "I had a woman I thought was a great sitter," says one mother, "until I found she spanked my child for wetting his pants. I got him out of there in a hurry."

• Look around the place. Is it basically clean? Is there a place for toys or are they all over the house? If it is a private home, ask the sitter where she keeps cleaning products and poisons and ask her to show them to you. If they are not totally beyond the reach of your baby (and beyond what he will be able to reach in another year or so), don't let him stay there.

For older preschoolers:

• Day care for the older preschooler, one who has been potty-trained, is essentially the same, except that the child of three years old and up can benefit greatly from being around other children in a social situation.

• Again, choose the day-care home or center *carefully*. For your peace of mind, it's worth taking the time to check references and visit the facilities.

• Who greets you at the door? If you *died*, would she make a good mother for your child? (The question may sound a bit extreme, but remember that this person will be caring for your child for many hours each day.)

• What kinds of toys and games do you see? Is television the only entertainment?

• What do the kids get for lunch?

• How do the children act toward one another? Are they kind or are they mean?

• Is there a familylike atmosphere?

- Look for *cleanliness*. Are the children clean, or do they have dirty faces and hands?
- Are any of the children off in a corner, looking sad and lonely?
- Does your child look forward to going back?
- How do they handle *discipline*? Are their methods of discipline similar to yours?
- How do the care-givers respond to accidents? Are they calm?
- Personally talk with every person who will be caring for your child.
- Give your child *time* to fit in and adjust. It takes from one week to two months for a child to adjust to a new day-care situation. Don't yank the child out and hop around from day care to day care. That is very hard for your child. Expect the "two week" syndrome. After about two weeks in a new day-care situation, your child may start to complain. That is normal. The newness has worn off; now he needs to settle in to the routine.

What If a Child Is Sick?

A child's becoming ill is the nightmare of the working mother, and there is no easy answer for it. Most new mothers probably tend to be too panicky rather than not cautious enough, but it might help to remember some basic information.

Usually a baby is not prone to colds and flu up to the age of six months, but after that age upper respiratory infections can be common. Because the Eustachian tubes are not well developed, babies and toddlers can get frequent ear infections, which can develop serious complications if left untreated.

Actually, one of the reasons that mothers are able to go to work is the fact that modern medicine can control so many of the terrible child-killing diseases of the past.

For example, a strep infection or scarlet fever, before the

era of penicillin, might have caused a child to be critically ill and could have taken his life. The development of effective antibiotics has helped bring under control infections that, in former years, would have required weeks or even months of constant nursing care.

Many young mothers have never seen the effects of such terrible diseases as polio and diphtheria, which now can be virtually eliminated by innoculation. Don't neglect your child's immunizations; make sure he has all of the protection available.

Protect Your Job

A sick child causes a working mother two kinds of anxiety: she worries because her child is ill, and she fears losing her job.

Most bosses are compassionate about sick children and will understand if the mother must miss work. The most benevolent boss, however, will get upset if the situation becomes chronic and the mother misses work frequently.

To avoid alienating your boss:

• Figure out a backup system. Many times children are not really seriously ill—they just don't feel well enough to go to school or to the sitter's. If they have a cold or flu they might infect other children. Try to find several persons you can call upon to stay with your child in that situation. Of course if the child is seriously ill, you will want to be with him, but if the illness is not serious, your backup system can save your job.

For example, one woman has two daughters who are pre-schoolers. When the first one came home from the sitter's with chicken pox, she knew that the other one would probably break out with them too. She knew that if she missed three weeks of work she would lose her job. At that time she did not have a backup system, so she took off two days from work and spent them on the telephone, trying to find someone willing to care for sick children. She finally found two older women who could alternate days. After that experience she made sure that she always had several names of emergency "pinch hitters."

If a grandmother lives nearby, she might be glad to be part of your backup system. A neighbor whose children are in school might be available to help. What about your husband? Would his job allow him to stay with the sick child part of the time?

• If you must miss work, be honest in your estimation of how long it will be before you return. To say you will probably be back tomorrow (when you know it will be a week) will just cause hard feelings.

• Offer to take work home. If you can keep up with part of the work at home, the others in the office will be less upset about their overload.

• Never leave work without the next day's jobs being outlined on your desk in the event a substitute might be brought in to cover for you. Leave a note for the substitute, giving your home telephone number, if possible. You will find that the habit of outlining a "Things to Do" list for the next day will benefit your own work, whether or not you have to stay home, because you will be better organized.

Notes

1 Tim LaHaye and Beverly LaHaye, "Working Mother vs. Homemaker," *Good News Broadcaster,* January 1980, p. 11.
2 Connie Rae, "Women Are Different," *Today's Christian Woman,* Fall/Winter 1978-79, p. 85.
3 Niki Scott, "Working Women," *The Indianapolis Star,* 9 December 1979.
4 Elizabeth Pope Frank, "Who's Minding the Children?" *Good Housekeeping,* February 1979, p. 111.

Suggested Reading

Henry Brandt and Phil Landrum, *I Want to Enjoy My Children* (Grand Rapids: Zondervan, 1977).

The Womanly Art of Breastfeeding (Chicago: LaLeche League, Int'l, 1958, 1963). It is possible to work full time and breastfeed your baby. Write LaLeche League International, 9616 Minneapolis Avenue, Franklin Park, IL 60131 (Telephone: 312-455-7730).

Chapter Four

Those Growing-up Years

Every mother who suffers through the anxiety of finding day care for a preschooler longs for the day when the child is safely tucked away in first grade.

"It will be so easy, then," she fantasizes. "He'll be in school *all day long.*"

She quickly discovers that enrolling a child in school does not solve her problems. They simply become different problems.

The basic difficulty, of course, is that the working day usually extends beyond school hours. Frequently children get home from school at 2:30 P.M. and stay alone until 6:00 P.M. or even later.

One divorced mother reports in a *Family Circle* survey that she has to leave her six children at home after school alone, but she worries about them.

"There are just too many things that can and do happen. Sometimes when an ambulance or fire engine passes the office, I tremble. . . . I have no one to listen to my fears and I worry a lot. If I paid a sitter it wouldn't make sense for me to work."[1]

Of the mothers who responded to the *Family Circle* survey, nearly 30 percent of those having children aged six to thirteen reported leaving their children home alone or with brothers or sisters after school. Another 15 percent left the question unanswered, which suggests that they had no appropriate child-care arrangements to report. It was estimated, then, that 45 percent of the children might stay at home by themselves.

However, reports *Family Circle*, "not one woman in a hundred would leave her children alone if she had any choice."[2]

Another mother described her neighborhood as filled with "bands of kids just at the age where they want to be 'in' with their friends, alone with temptations and dozens of empty houses—I wonder what society will be like when these children who have grown up with so little care and guidance are in charge of the country."

Mothers are not the only ones who worry. Urie Bronfenbrenner, Cornell University psychology professor, has taken the unpopular stance that there are real dangers to the family when both parents are working long hours.

"Increasing numbers of children," says Bronfenbrenner, "are coming home to empty houses. If there's any reliable predictor of trouble, it probably begins with children coming home to an empty house, whether the problem is reading difficulties, truancy, dropping out, drug addiction or childhood depression."[3]

Bronfenbrenner has come to the frightening conclusion that the needs of this nation's youngsters are met "less and less effectively each year."[4]

Other Options?

In some areas, more options are open to mothers who do not want their school-age children to go home to an empty house. It is increasingly popular for elementary schools to offer an after-class program for the children whose mothers work. Many day-care centers take elementary-school-age children both before and after school, and in some areas the school bus picks up the day-care children in the morning and takes them back after school. Some Headstart programs also fill that need.

The problem for many women is that there is no day-care center in a convenient location, or else they are concerned about the quality of day care that is available.

Some neighborhoods have mothers who help other women by providing after-school crafts and games in their homes for the children of the working mothers. They have found that a good way to earn some extra money while helping their friends. Not every neighborhood has a person willing to do that, however.

The basic reason so many children are left alone is *money*. "If I had to pay someone to watch the kids," says one mother, "it would end up *costing* me to work. I like working, but not *that much*." So kids will continue to come home to empty houses.

Referee with a Telephone

When children are home unsupervised, one serious problem for the parent is having to referee their inevitable fights.

"When it gets to the point where they call me at work," says one mother, "if there is a suggestion I can make I will, but usually I *hiss* and tell them to leave each other alone. Unfortunately, you can't spank a kid over the phone!"

Only rarely does it get bad enough that she has to leave work early to go home and break it up. "If I do go home, she warns, "they'd better be bleeding or have something broken!"

She goes on to say that most problems of that kind can be avoided if the children have something to do after school.

"Usually, their fights are the result of boredom. I try to have something that they will enjoy doing when they get home—to take the pressure off. Now that they are older, they sometimes make cookies or fudge. Sometimes I leave out graham crackers and the ingredients and instructions for making a simple icing. That is fun for them."

Another mothers says, "I feel really guilty about not being there to greet the enthusiastic children coming home from school. I have tried to make up for it by giving them a call about the time that they get home, but it sometimes backfires. Instead of a happy, friendly conversation I get a tattletale report on the brother or sister. That I can do without. They know they can call me if they want to, but they know it had better be a friendly conversation."

Baseball and Music

Elizabeth and David have two boys and a girl in elementary school. She works about thirty hours a week as a cashier, and her schedule changes from week to week. She works many evenings. He is just starting on a new job as a real estate salesman, and he works long hours and never knows if he will get home for supper or not.

They live several miles out of town, and that has caused problems. The boys want to play baseball, but they haven't yet been able to work out the myriad problems involved in getting them to practices and games. Their daughter wants to take piano lessons, but they never can depend on being free at a certain time each week.

So Elizabeth and David feel bad about it, but at the present there is nothing they can do. She would like to get a job with regular hours, but she cannot find anything that pays as well as what she does now. They hope to move into town so that the children can get to ball practice and music lessons, at least, on their bicycles.

Many families have sadly concluded that extracurricular activities must be eliminated. Even when the transportation problems are worked out, piano lessons are often dropped when it becomes evident that most kids need supervised practicing. What frequently happens is that a child will start taking lessons, but neither Mom nor Dad is at home when the practicing is supposedly being done. The child quickly discovers that he can get away without really practicing. Soon discouragement sets in, and the child wonders why piano playing is so difficult. So that's the end of piano. Homework problems can also happen the same way.

School Problems

When neither parent is available during the day, school problems sometimes result. Often parent-teacher conferences are missed, and frequently communications break down. Notes sent home from school about a small problem can be lost in the shuffle, and the delay produces a big problem. Then the mother or father has to take time off from work for a special conference.

School vacations and snow days are also headaches. The solution in most cases is a friend in the neighborhood who will watch children of mothers who work, but it still is a worry.

Summer Blues

Summertime is another bad time for the mother who works all year. What can you do with kids who are home all day?

The obvious solution is to hire a teenager who is also out of school, with too much time and too little money. Sometimes that solution works; other times it is a disaster.

"The biggest problem," says one mother, "is finding someone dependable. Most teenagers are just not mature enough to stay committed to the very demanding job of taking care of three kids, feeding them two meals a day, and not letting the house be in shambles when you get home. Not many sixteen-year-old kids are ready for that kind of commitment."

Another mother got around the problem by hiring two sitters, sisters who would share the job by alternating days or even parts of the day. That plan helped the girls feel less trapped by their job, so that they could also enjoy their summer.

Some communities are seeking to solve the child-care problems by coordinating efforts with the local park and recreation department and using the school facilities to provide all-day child care.

In Falls Church, Virginia, the League of Women Voters developed the Falls Church Extended Day Care program, which provides both before- and after-school care and a complete summer program. Linda Clinton reports in *Working Mother* that on a typical day the children might be roller-skating in the morning, taking part in a draw-your-pet contest, eating a bag lunch brought from home (milk is provided), playing basketball in the afternoon, enjoying a snack, and, finally, trying their hands at making delicate tissue-paper flowers to take home to their mothers.[5]

That program sounds wonderful, especially to those millions of parents who have no such option available. I cannot help but believe that the local church is missing a good opportunity to serve the community and at the same time bring boys and girls to a saving knowledge of the Lord Jesus Christ. Wouldn't it be great if our day-care problems could be met, not by government, but by the local churches? Perhaps your church has the facilities to operate that kind of program.

The Home Is a Filling Station?

Michigan State University professor William Lazer makes the grim prediction that "the home will become a filling station for peoples' needs." A General Electric executive states, "The family meal is a thing of the past. It's going the way of the family breakfast and the family lunch."[6]

When the woman was at home during the day, it was a bit easier for her to be a stabilizing influence on the family, because she had more time to keep things running smoothly and to do the "nice things" that make a house a home.

As I talked with women in all sorts of jobs, I found most of them very concerned about their families and homes. Several expressed alarm at the "catch as catch can" direction into which their own households were drifting.

"We haven't sat down together for the evening meal," says one mother, "since I started to work. The kids have meetings or ball practice every night of the week, and I don't get home until six. They are usually gone before I get home."

As this mother described the way they have their evening meals, visions of filling stations danced through my head.

"I usually cook the meat and vegetables and fix a salad the night before and put it all in the refrigerator. Then as each one gets home, he or she will put some meat and vegetables on a plate, warm them up in the microwave, and dish out a little salad. That's all there is to it. Most of the time each person eats alone, although the television is probably on."

What can be done to protect the family? To keep the house a home even when both parents are working?

> Unless the LORD builds the house,
> its builders labor in vain. . . .
> In vain you rise early
> and stay up late,
> toiling for food to eat—
>
> Psalm 127:1-2, NIV*

Whenever you are making a change in your family situation, such as taking a job or taking a more demanding job, you need to consider the cost. Will it be worth it? You may be working hard—rising up early and staying up late—for material things: a nice house, another car, or some other thing. But unless the *Lord* builds your house, you are doing it in vain. You *can* work at a job outside the home. That is not the determining factor. The important thing is this—is the Lord the center of your household?

New International Version.

Family Time

If both parents have outside jobs, extra effort must be made to have daily family time. That is a time set aside every day for the family to be together. Kids are never too young or too old for family time. Family time has three purposes:

- *Communication.* Each member of the family can share something of his or her life with the rest of the family. To get conversation started, ask, "What is the best thing that happened today?" Give each person time to relate his or her "best thing."

- *Devotions.* Family time gives an opportunity for parents to teach the children to spend time in God's Word each day.

- *Prayer.* Family time is essential for learning about each other's needs and praying together for them.

Some jobs, because of the traveling or late hours required, make it impossible for the family to be together all during the week. Many husbands and wives work opposite shifts, so that one of them can be home with the children. During the week, it seems, those husbands and wives are like ships that pass in the night. It may be impossible at this point to have a daily family time, but at the very least you should set aside some time together on the weekend. Make it a matter of prayer. It may be that God will make an adjustment to give you at least one hour together each day.

If you are a single mother or your husband is gone all week in a traveling job, then you should go ahead and establish family time. Family time should take place even if one or more members of the family are not at home.

Keep in mind as you read this that family time is short—no more than fifteen minutes need be spent for the devotional part.

You and your husband should establish some ground rules in order to make the family time work. For example:

• *Determine to have family time.* Establish it as a top priority. If you have family time after supper, television is *off* during and after the meal, until you are finished with family time. No telephone calls are accepted (unless business or long distance). Mom or Dad answers the telephone and takes a message.

• *Have a happy atmosphere.* Family time is *not* the time to bring up bad things about any family member. Do not use family time to point out each child's failures and weaknesses in the name of "teaching." That will make him or her hate family time. A special effort should be made to say something positive and encouraging to each family member. Don't allow criticism or complaint. If someone has a grievance, or a sibling squabble is going on, get it settled *before* family time or set a time to deal with it later. (If squabbling can cause a delay in family time or cause it to be canceled, the kids will use that technique to try to boycott it!) They will eventually like this time, but it might take a while.

• *Keep it short.* If you try to cover too much at once, the children will get fidgety. Ten to fifteen minutes is about right. For very small children, five minutes is enough.

• *Let the children participate.* The children like to take an active part by doing part of the reading, asking or answering questions, and so on.

• *Keep it fun.* The Christian life is to be enjoyed, not endured!

• *Keep it varied.* Avoid the rut of always doing the same thing.

• *Pray for each other.* As lines of communication open, you will find that family members are sometimes facing problems. What a joy it is to be able to pray for basketball practice, a math test, or a problem a friend is facing. Be open enough with your children to pray about some of your own problems at work and in your life. It will help them realize that problems are a part of life and that we can ask the Lord's help in dealing with them.

Memory-Makers

Children remember for all their lifetimes the "special moments" together. Special holidays and birthdays can continue to be celebrated, even if Mom is working. An occasion can be made festive by lighting some candles and getting out the good dishes.

Sometimes working mothers try to relieve their guilt by making every moment at home totally child-centered and memorable. That is not practical or healthy for the child. If every day you bring home a present or take him to the zoo, pretty soon he will *demand* that you drum up some excitement for him.

The real memory-makers for children are those quiet moments together. Your activities need not be something expensive or dramatic—just taking a walk together and looking at the sunset can mean much to the child and to you.

The Great Put Off

Most working mothers are very concerned about the needs of the children but too often find themselves participating in what one mother sees as the Great Put Off. In *Better Homes and Gardens* she laments, "I don't have the time to go on that field trip with your class. I can't go to the library with you. You need a cardboard box 2½ feet high and 14 inches wide for a history project? Sorry. You have a cold and want me to come home from work? I can't, but drink lots of orange juice and stay in bed. You missed the bus, forgot your lunch, gym clothes, need a ride to . . . cheerleading practice? Sorry, I'm busy. You want to have friends over tonight? You can't—the house is a mess. You didn't make the team? You failed a test? Your friends are angry with you? Sorry, I'm busy . . . I don't have the time . . . that's too bad . . . We will have to talk about it sometime."[7]

You need to take an honest look at your children's needs and your responsibility toward them. Some of the problems can be solved by better planning. Do the demands of your job *fit* into family life right now? Perhaps another kind of work would give you more flexibility. In some cases the whole issue of "Should I be working at all?" may need to be reconsidered.

On the other hand, don't heap guilt feelings upon yourself. If kids know they can make mother feel guilty, they seem to enjoy doing that very thing. Get organized, do what you can, and don't give yourself ulcers over what you can't do.

Fatigue and Time Pressure

Two of the greatest enemies of family life in these busy times seem to be *fatigue* and *time pressure*. It is not just parents who are busy. Kids are busy, too, with music, sports, school, homework, and all their other activities. To combat fatigue, *get organized* and *go to bed*. Getting organized will help you sleep better, because you won't be worrying about all the things you have left undone. To combat time pressure, give some thought to the family's activities. What can be dropped? You may find yourselves overcommitted to too many different things. Eliminate some of them. You can't possibly do everything that attracts you, and neither can your children. Help them to learn to make choices.

Changing Gears

The hardest part of the day may be the moment that you get back with the children after being away from them all day. Changing gears from "businessperson" to "mommy" is often not an easy transition to make. The kids probably get along with the sitter just fine, but as soon as Mom is in sight, they start howling and wailing and giving details of the day's every squabble. Back in the olden days, Mom would threaten,

"Wait till your father gets home." Now, because it's "Wait till your *mother* gets home," all the day's troubles are unloaded on Mom the moment she enters the door.

"When I read in the magazines," says one mother, "about the women who come home from work and glide into the bathroom to take a hot bubble bath and lie down for an hour, I have to laugh. There's no way I can do that. The kids need me during that hour. I've been away from them all day! How can I shut them off and go take a bubble bath?"

One thing that seems to help many women is establishing a coming-home ritual. One woman says that every evening she has a tea party for herself and her children. She makes sure that she includes some nutritious snacks and different kinds of tea on her shopping list.

The children are informed that they must wait until tea time to tell Mommy about their day. The moment she gets home she puts the tea water on, then quickly changes into comfortable clothes. She even has a special little tablecloth that she uses just for this purpose. Then they all gather around the table and have their tea with a snack and talk about what happened that day.

"I've learned that if I want my children to communicate with me I must *stop* what I'm doing, *sit down*, and look into the eyes of the person talking. If I don't, the child will assume I'm not really that interested.

"It's during our tea time," says this mother, "that I can unwind and gear down from the office. It's also during this time that I hear about problems with friends, school difficulties, and other traumas of a child's day. It allows me to give the children my fullest attention, before we have to turn to our evening responsibilities."

We must not listen to those who would say that these growing-up years are less important just because they represent a lull between the storms of the "twos" and the "teens." Vital things are happening in the children's lives as they are growing, maturing, and becoming more responsible.

Notes

[1] Jane Whitbread, "Who's Taking Care of the Children?" *Family Circle*, 20 February 1979, p. 92. Reprinted from the Feb. 20, 1979 issue of Family Circle Magazine. © 1979, THE FAMILY CIRCLE, INC. All rights reserved.

[2] Ibid.

[3] Urie Brofenbrenner and Susan Byrne, "Nobody Home: The Erosion of the American Family, *Psychology Today,* May 1977, p. 41.

[4] From "Impact at Home When Mother Takes a Job," a copyrighted interview in *U.S. News & World Report,* 15 January, 1979, p. 69.

[5] Linda Clinton, "A Town with a Summer Solution," *Working Mother,* July 1979, p. 24.

[6] "How Life's Pulse Will Change in Next 10 Years," *U.S. News & World Report,* 15 October 1979, p. 52.

[7] Kate Keating, "Are Working Mothers Attempting Too Much?" *Better Homes and Gardens,* October 1978, p. 27. © 1978 Meredith Corp. Used by permission.

Suggested Reading

Elva Anson and Kathie Liden, *The Compleat Family Book* (Chicago: Moody, 1979).

D. Ross Campbell, *How to Really Love Your Child* (Wheaton, Ill.: Victor, 1979).

Kenneth Taylor, *Devotions for the Children's Hour* (Chicago: Moody, 1954, 1968). This fine book is designed to help children understand basic truths about God and what it means to know Him.

Our Daily Bread is an excellent devotional for family use. To get on the mailing list (free of charge) write: Radio Bible Class, Box 22, Grand Rapids, MI 49555.

The Ready-Set-Grow Series, written by Joy Wilt and published by Word (Waco, Tex.), very helpfully deals with the problems kids face. Use these books in addition to Bible reading and devotions, not in place of them. Our family usually takes several weeks with one book, going over only a few pages each evening. The titles include: *A Kid's Guide to Making Friends; A Kid's Guide to Managing Money; Handling Your Ups and Downs; Keeping Your Body Alive and Well; Making Up Your Own Mind; Mine and Yours; Needing Each Other; Nitty-Gritty of Family Life, The; Saying What You Mean; Surviving Fights with your Brothers and Sisters; You're All Right;* and *You're One of a Kind.*

Cassette Tapes

James Dobson, "Preparing for Adolescence," Vision House, 1507 E. McFadden, Santa Ana, CA 92705. Six tapes.

Chapter Five

Teens Need Parenting, Too

Phyllis Anderson shrugs. She speaks slowly with a North Carolina twang. A lock of hair falls on her forehead, and she brushes it back impatiently.

"I tried," she says. "I really did. Billy was such a sweet little boy. If I had known things would turn out like this—" Her voice trails off as she takes a sip of too-hot coffee from a Styrofoam cup.

We are in the back room of the beauty shop where she works. The smell of permanent wave lotion fills the air, and the chatter of women is an incessant drone, interrupted occasionally by a shrill laugh. She speaks with a forced hoarseness above the clatter in the next room, her voice revealing the strain.

She tells Billy's story.

Billy was a quiet little tyke in elementary school. He didn't say much and didn't get in trouble with the teachers. He started having problems in school in second grade. He just couldn't seem to learn to read. When the teachers would call on him, he would mumble and stammer. The other kids snickered. Finally the teachers stopped calling on him at all. At recess he played alone, watching the others from a distance.

Phyllis had been working part time at a gift shop since Billy was a baby. However, she believed she could make more money if she developed a skill, and she had always enjoyed fixing her hair in different ways. When she finally got the nerve to ask her husband, Bill, about going to beauty school, all he wanted to know was if she could pay for it out of her earnings at the gift shop. It took a while to save enough, but she finally got the money she needed.

The day that she started to school was one of those wet, drizzly autumn days. She was rushing around the kitchen trying to get breakfast fixed before Bill came down.

"Mommy," a small voice whined, "can you help me?"

"Not now, Billy," she said harshly. "I don't have time!"

Bill came into the kitchen just at that moment. "So this is what it's gonna be, huh? A whining kid and a screaming wife. Other women seem to manage everything without falling apart. And where's breakfast?"

The skillet was on the stove, empty.

He glared at Phyllis and stormed out of the room. The slamming door exploded in her ears. Billy looked at her mournfully, then put on his jacket and quietly left for school, face unwashed and hair uncombed.

The more resentful Bill was of her work and school, the more determined Phyllis became. *He's not going to hold me back,* she thought bitterly.

She was gone long hours working and studying. Many times Billy was at home alone. But he was so quiet that she didn't worry about him. *I'm lucky to have such a good-natured kid,* she often thought. His grades were always low, but Phyllis just thought, *Oh, well. I'm no genius myself.* She was too busy, and Bill didn't care enough to go to a PTA meeting or conference with Billy's teachers.

Phyllis became totally wrapped up in what was now her career. She surprised even herself with her ability to create hairstyles. To her astonishment she loved the difficult material she was required to learn, especially the anatomy and chemistry.

Because she did so well in school, she got a job with an exclusive shop in a nearby city. She entered every available contest and won trips to New York to learn the latest styles. She began to make money, and that was what she and Bill mostly fought about.

"*Another* new dress?" he yelled. "What do you think you are—some kind of hoity-toity *lady*, for crying out loud? If you'd stay home once in a while you'd see that other people besides you would like some new things."

She was actually relieved when Bill moved out. *I can get along just fine without him,* she fumed to herself. Billy, as usual, said nothing.

By now he was fourteen years old, a silent, unhappy boy. Phyllis did not know how miserable he was.

She was surprised one day when he expressed an interest in taking art lessons. An art teacher at school had told him that he had talent and that he should take some private instruction. Billy asked Phyllis about it on a day when she was exhausted and irritable.

"*Art* lessons?" she shrieked. "Are you kidding? That's all I need—something else to worry about. I don't have time the way it is to get everything done around here. And I sure don't have time to cart you around to art lessons."

He never mentioned it again.

Phyllis was gone long hours every day, but she noticed a subtle change in Billy. Instead of being silent, he became surly. He began making friends, and Phyllis was glad until she saw the rough-looking, tough-talking kids who became his buddies.

She began calling from work in the afternoons to see if he was home. No, it was more to see if he was home *alone*.

He began staying out late at night. She told him to be in by ten. Once, he came in at midnight and she screamed at him.

He screamed back at her, sounding, she thought heavily, just like Bill. The next night it was eleven when he got in, but she was at a meeting and didn't get home until after he did. After that, he just ignored her.

She realized she had lost control of him. When she found marijuana in his dresser drawer, she sensed impending doom. But she was not prepared for the night she found him in bed, unconscious. He had taken an overdose of her sleeping pills.

"Dear Mom," his note said, "you'll be better off without me." He had sketched in the corner a picture of a sad-eyed boy hugging a puppy.

Phyllis was overcome by feelings of guilt. *I made him feel that way*, she thought. *I've always been too busy for him, and now I've lost him.*

Billy did recover, but he remained depressed and sullen. He rejected all of Phyllis's attempts to make things up to him. The harder she tried, the more he withdrew into a shell. Phyllis was living in fear that he would try to take his life again.

"Oh, God," she cried out, "can you help us? Is it too late?"

Is It Too Late?

Phyllis and Billy are in the midst of incredible trauma. Phyllis wants to help Billy, but she does not know what to do. She feels helpless and lonesome and very much afraid. Mostly she is afraid that it's too late.

The teenage years are emotionally charged, difficult years at best. The fact that Phyllis is working is obviously not the only problem in this home. The family members evidently have never communicated with each other very well, and the home lacks a spiritual foundation.

Like Phyllis, many parents may wonder if it is too late. Can any parenting in those teenage years make up for failure in the past?

There is hope, even in a situation as difficult as this one.

But the hope lies in the *power of God* to transform people's lives, because that is what is needed in this family and millions of others. "Turning over a new leaf" will not be enough to get to the root problem, because it is a *spiritual* problem. It requires a spiritual solution.

No problem is too big for God.

Emotional Years

The teenage years are well known for being an emotional, upsetting, and difficult time. They are also the years when the mothers of the teenagers seem to become more involved in outside interests, whether it is a job, volunteer work, or a Christian ministry of some kind. During those years, parents themselves are not immune from emotional upheaval. Men may feel a sense of panic about their careers, thinking that the years are slipping by too quickly and it is "now or never." Some women, on the other hand, begin to resent the loss of youth, and that resentment can be magnified by the presence of a beautiful daughter coming into the full bloom of womanhood. The years are complex at best.

One mother of teenagers shocked her family by announcing that she was no longer going to do the dirty work around the house. "I'm going to get a job where I can be appreciated for a change."

Another mother worked her way up from the position of teller and became branch manager of a large metropolitan bank just at the time her children entered the teenage years. She also felt the need to take some college courses, so she is now away from home three evenings a week. She is divorced, the teenagers are home alone, and she feels uneasy about it.

"It doesn't bother me being away from home during the day. The kids are involved in so many activities and that time is fairly well structured. What really worries me is being gone in the evenings. The kids are very self-sufficient. They know how to cook and clean and take care of themselves. But in some

ways I think they need me more now than when they were
little. They are making choices and decisions now that will
affect their entire lives. I feel I need to be there to help guide
them in making those decisions."

A high school English teacher who has teenagers of her own
says, "I can tell right away the kids in my classes whose parents really care about them and the ones who are more or less
left to fend for themselves. It's not just a question of a
mother's working. Some mothers don't have jobs but are so
wrapped up in clubs and volunteer work that they aren't available to their kids, either. It seems to get down to priorities
and making choices based on the good of the family rather
than thinking first of the woman's own personal achievement."

One mother made a decision that was hard. She had been
admitted to a five-year program to study architecture, which
was quite an achievement in itself. The program was very
demanding and would require many hours of work and study
every day.

"Just as I was about ready to enter the program," she says,
"I looked again at the kids. One was a sophomore, the other a
senior in high school. In three years they would both be gone,
and I would have all kinds of time to study. In some ways our
kids need us more in their teen years than any other time. I
didn't want to be unavailable to them if they really needed
me. So I compromised. I'm working three days a week for an
architect. When our younger son graduates, I'll get back in a
program. I feel good about the decision. I just know in my
heart it was the right thing to do."

How Important Are Families?

Not long ago *U.S. News and World Report* interviewed a
number of top students to get their impressions of their
families and the way they perceive the importance of their
relationships with their parents. Here are two of their com-

ments, which show that families are still important.

A young man, seventeen, from Los Angeles: "I have an excellent relationship with my parents. We all have chores to be done at home. We can't watch TV during the week nights at all. My parents provided me with morals and values. I'm going to live the way I'd live if I still had them telling me: 'You can't go out that late.' "

A girl, also seventeen, from Detroit: "The rules in my family are pretty strict. We sit down to dinner together every night as a family. We're expected in a certain time at night and we call if we're going to be late."[1]

• All kids, especially teens, need love and approval. They are insecure, for the most part, and very intimidated by their peers. Let them know that you approve of them. You may not always approve of their *behavior*, but approve of *them* as very special people. Be honest with them, and don't be afraid to admit your mistakes to them.

• Do everything possible to help each child develop one skill or talent in which he or she can really excel. Doing something really well builds self-esteem. That will take *time*, *inconvenience*, and probably *money*. Because of your job you may think, *It's just impossible to get him to lessons. I don't have time to see that he practices. We'll just have to forget it.* Before you give up, really check out all avenues. It is very important.

• Your teenager needs limits set and rules enforced. I asked one mother whose teenage daughter was home by herself every afternoon if the girl had ever had boyfriends in the house after school. The mother winced.

"That issue is a constant source of argument. We have a rule that she is not to have a boyfriend in the house without her father or myself. I know that it would be entirely too cozy, and her reputation would be hurt if we allowed it. If it ever became a real problem, and I found that she didn't obey the rule, we would have to make some drastic changes. She might

get an after-school job if it seemed she had too much time on
her hands. If necessary, I would quit my job. So far, she is so
busy with activities after school that things have stayed on an
even keel. But, believe me, it's not easy!"

• Make sure that you are available to your teenager. That
may mean postponing for a while some things you would like
to do. Can those things wait? Your teenager can't.

• Don't believe that your teenager no longer needs parenting. He or she is living through an emotionally-charged time
of life and needs you to help him or her deal with it. God gives
children parents to love them, guide them, and encourage
them through those times. You may be operating only as a
lifeguard at a swimming pool, standing along the sidelines.
The lifeguard doesn't jump into the water until there is trouble, but he'd better be there at the first sign of a problem. If
the lifeguard notices a *potential* problem, he doesn't just ignore it. He counsels, teaches, sets guidelines, and makes certain the rules are obeyed. That is the hard job of being the
parent of a teenager: standing by, watching, patiently waiting,
hoping you won't be needed, but being available if you are.

Phyllis and Billy

A number of months passed before I saw Phyllis in the
beauty shop again. I could not believe the change in her. She
was actually smiling. I was a little reluctant to bring up a sad
subject, because she looked so happy, but I asked her how
Billy was doing.

"You know," she said, "I think he's going to be all right. I
finally realized that I was no good to him or anybody or anything else as long as I was so torn up over it all. Finally I just
let go. I just put him into God's care.

"I had been doing a lot of thinking about spiritual things. A
friend of mine told me that I should try prayer, because I'd
tried everything else.

"I just told God that I want Him to be real to me. I couldn't handle all this by myself. Another friend invited me to go to church with her, so I did. I heard all these wonderful things about Jesus and how He had died for me. I had gone with her several times when one day it all suddenly made sense to me. "In my mind I saw Jesus. He was suffering. Bleeding. Dying. He was dying for *me*. He had to die, because there's no way I could be good enough on my own to be acceptable to God. I realized that if I had been the only person who had ever lived, He would have died for me. I was ready to open my heart to Him, to have Him take control of my life. At the end of the service they gave an invitation, and I almost ran down the aisle. What Jesus had done for me was almost more than I could bear! I accepted Him as my Savior right then.

"I felt a wonderful peace in my heart, but the situation at home was still rough. Billy was very unpleasant to live with, blaming his father and me for his problems. The Lord began working within me to change some of my bad attitudes, but I grew very impatient. I said, 'Hey, Lord, *I'm* not the one who needs changing around here. Billy's the one you need to work on!' Finally I realized that my own resentment was sin that I needed to confess. Change had to start with someone, and it might as well be me. I told him about the decision I had made to receive Christ, but he just sneered at me. I didn't push. I just told him that I would pray for him.

"A number of months have passed. I enrolled Billy in an art program for high school kids at a local university. It is funded through a federal grant, so it was not expensive. I drive him to his lessons every Tuesday night. The instructor tells me he has real talent.

"I'm trying to be more available and sensitive to him, too. Even though I still work many hours a day, I block out time for him so that we can have more time together.

"I've not yet convinced him to go to church with me. I hate it so much that all those early years passed without his having the opportunity of learning about God and meeting Christian friends. But I know that God meets us at the point of our need, and, ultimately, He works out everything for good for those who love Him. I'll keep on praying for Billy.

"I just thank the Lord that He has given me peace in my heart. When I start to worry again, I just remember Isaiah 26:3: 'Thou wilt keep him in perfect peace, whose mind is stayed on thee: because he trusteth in thee.' "*

Notes

[1] From "What Kids Are Saying About Their Parents," a copyrighted article in *U.S. News & World Report,* 14 November 1977, pp. 89-90.

*King James Version.

Chapter Six

Freud, Guilt, and Motherhood

Marsha Miller is busy getting supper on the table. *Funny,* she thinks as she gets milk from the refrigerator, *there's a lot of lunch meat left. I'm surprised the boys would take peanut butter and jelly.*

Her thoughts are interrupted by the telephone ringing.

"Mrs. Miller?" questions a businesslike voice. "This is Paul Anderson, principal of School Fifty-three."

The principal! The boys must be in trouble!

"Now I don't want to alarm you, but there's something you might not know because you work. Your boys have gone without lunch every day this week."

No lunch! It wraps Marsha like a straitjacket, that horrible feeling known to every mother: guilt.

Sheila hated to leave Susie at home that morning. She had complained of stomach pains in the night, but by morning she seemed a little better. The other children left for school, and Susie assured her mother that she would be all right. So Sheila went to work, worried, but convinced that Susie had the twenty-four-hour flu.

Susie called at work an hour later. "Mommy, it really hurts."

"Just lie down on the couch, honey. I'll be home in a few hours."

After lunch, Sheila called home. There was no answer. Panicky, she called her husband's office. No, the secretary said, he had been out all day. She tried the home number again and let it ring twenty-seven times.

She grabbed her coat and quickly told her supervisor the problem. It seemed to take hours to get home.

"Susie! Susie!" she yelled through the house. No answer. She raced upstairs and found Susie sprawled on the bathroom floor, her face as white as her nightgown. She had fallen and had hit her head.

She regained consciousness as Sheila scooped her up and ran with her to the car. At the emergency room the problem was diagnosed as a ruptured appendix, and she was rushed upstairs to surgery.

Sheila sat down in the telephone booth and sobbed. *I should have known it was something serious*, she thought. *Why did I leave her alone? Why? Why? If I'd been at home I would have known she was really sick.*

All mothers, whether we are at home or employed feel guilt at times. Sometimes we feel guilty because we are guilty. At times we really do fail and need to ask God's forgiveness. Other times we are not really guilty—we just feel guilty. There are two main reasons for those unwarranted feelings of guilt: the Victorian image of the "perfect" mother, and Freudian psychology. Those two forces affect our thinking today more than we realize.

The "Perfect" Mother

It was during the Victorian era that "motherhood" became romanticized beyond reality. Women were put on a pedestal and their natural functions of bearing children and nurturing the young were idealized. A woman was told that there was something magical about giving birth, that having a baby would transform her into the loving, self-sacrificing, perfect mother she had always hoped to be. Also during that time fathers began abdicating the parenting role. After all, if mothers were so perfect, shouldn't they do all the parenting? Besides, that would give men more time to make money. It seemed reasonable.

Before long the mother found herself isolated, all alone with the big job of raising the children. The father became a figurehead, king of his castle in name only. As far as the children were concerned, mother was clearly in charge.

Freud Adds More Guilt

Sigmund Freud opened a new world in the study of personality development, and he stressed the importance of experiences in infancy and early childhood. He brought to the people the message that a child could be psychologically destroyed at a very early age. Because the mother was the one with the child most of the time, if something happened to the psyche, it was obviously her fault.

Betty Friedan in *The Feminine Mystique* eloquently reports that under the Freudian microscope mothers began to take the blame for every ill in society:

> Oedipus conflict and sibling rivalry became household words. Frustration was as great a peril to childhood as scarlet fever. And singled out for special attention was the "mother." It was suddenly discovered that the mother could be blamed for almost everything. In every case history of a troubled child, alcoholic, suicidal, schizophrenic, psychopathic, neurotic adult; impotent, homosexual male, frigid or promiscuous female; ulcerous, asthmatic and otherwise disturbed American, could be found a mother. A frustrated repressed, disturbed, martyred, never satisfied, unhappy woman. A demanding, nagging, shrewish wife. An objecting, overprotecting, dominating mother.[1]

The Bible nowhere teaches that mothers are perfect or that women are any less sinful than men. Women are designed by God to bear children and nurse the young. They generally are more tender and loving toward small children than men are.

But that does not mean that women are perfect or that they should be burdened with the total responsibility for the children. God gives each child two parents for a reason.

The "perfect mother" image is still with us. The manufacturers of Mother's Day cards love it, but the *real* mother panics as she realizes how far she is from that ideal.

When God was revealing His steadfastness to the Jewish people, He clearly stated that mothers are not perfect, for only He is perfect.

"Can a mother forget the baby at her breast and have no compassion on the child she has borne? *Though she may forget,* 1 will not forget you!" (Isaiah 49:15, NIV, emphasis mine).

The Bible also teaches that love, even a mother's love for her child, is not automatic. Older women are instructed in Titus 2:4 to teach the younger women to love their husbands and children! If "mother love" were automatic, we would not need to be taught.

Though Freudian psychology has been beneficial in pointing out the importance of early childhood, it also has given mothers an unhealthy sense of responsibility for a child's mental health and happiness. In fact, mothers have become hesitant to discipline children at all, fearful that discipline might cause frustration and damage to the psyche.

Now a mother not only had to be perfect herself but, according to the Freudian mandate, she had to raise perfectly well-adjusted children without frustrating them in any way. Clearly, she was set up for failure.

Untold numbers of women are entering the work force because they are disappointed in themselves as mothers and upset by the behavior of children. Contrary to the Victorian myth, a mother does not feel tender and loving when faced with a screaming baby, a whining toddler, or a sarcastic adolescent. What she feels much of the time is hostility, resentment, and fatigue. "I guess I'm just not the mothering type," she says as she searches the want ads.

Even by going to work, however, she cannot escape the "perfect" mother. She feels disapproval from mothers who do not work ("I am creating a perfect environment for my children—I would never let someone else raise them"), from her mother ("I stayed home with my children—that's where a mother belongs"), and from her children ("Jimmy's mom brought homemade chocolate chip cookies to the school party," or, "All the other mothers showed up for the school talent show").

God's Answer to Guilt

A mother's sense of guilt goes far beyond the fact that she is working or not working. Each mother must turn to God for guidance, and each mother must analyze her own motivations for working. The decision to work is between her and her family and God.

But once she has determined that working is right for her, and she still feels guilty, perhaps there is a valid reason for it.

It is possible that in some way your working has caused your children harm. Only you can know your situation. If you know that right now your working situation is hurting your children, take steps to make changes.

• If you have an incompetent sitter, change sitters.

• If your job does not allow you time to be with your children, look for a job that will.

• If you have taken on a job that is too demanding to handle along with your family, try to find one that has less pressure until your family's needs are less intense.

• If your children are preschool age and you believe that you should be with them during those years, talk to your husband about it and try to adjust your life-style so that you can.

Whatever you do, don't just go on and on feeling guilty. If you can change your circumstances, change them. If you can't change them, *accept* them, and go on from there.

Some feel guilty about events that are past or about failures of long ago. It is a waste of your energy and mental health to worry and feel guilty about them.

God has provided for us the Bible, which tells us how we can know Him and how we can be obedient to Him. The more obedient we are, the less guilt we will feel. God also has provided a way for us to incorporate into our daily lives the very qualities that make us more effective human beings, both as mothers and as workers. The more effective we are, the less guilt we will feel. But in the final analysis, the only solution for guilt is accepting God's forgiveness through Jesus Christ.

The Spirit-Controlled Life

The qualities of love, joy, peace, patience, kindness, goodness, faithfulness, gentleness, and self-control are traits that come from the Spirit of God. They are the "fruit" of allowing Him to be in control of the Christian's life. The Spirit of God comes to dwell within the believer at the moment that person receives Christ as Savior. He will never leave. However, as long as we live on this earth we will also have the self (the sinful nature), which has the *tendency* to sin. We can allow either the Holy Spirit or self to control us. The choice is ours to make. The Bible calls it being "filled with the Spirit" when we allow the Holy Spirit to be in control.

C. Sumner Wemp quotes a present-day Greek scholar as saying, "Being filled with the Spirit is not putting gas in the tank; it is putting a Driver at the wheel."[2]

So, living is something like driving an automobile:

Self is in the driver's seat, living for self, alienated from God.

Before a person becomes a Christian, he or she is controlled by self. This person has no spiritual life. He may try to be "religious," but he is living for self.

The *Holy Spirit* is in control. Self is out of the way. God is not the *passenger*, rather He is the *Driver*. Life is characterized by the fruit of the Spirit: love, joy, peace, patience, kindness, and so on.

The Holy Spirit enters the life when Jesus Christ is accepted. What is supposed to happen is that the believer yields the control of his life to the Holy Spirit, and self gets into the backseat.

Self is back in control. The Holy Spirit has been put into the backseat. The life lacks love, joy, peace, patience, kindness. It is characterized by worry, frustration, guilt, anxiety, irritability, grumbling, lack of contentment, quarreling.

Sadly, this third possibility describes the *majority* of Christians. Self takes control of the life once again, and the Holy Spirit is inactive in the backseat. God has as much power as ever, but we aren't "plugged into" His power unless He is in control. The Bible calls this Christian "carnal" (see 1 Corinthians 3:1-3).

What To Do?

The remedy for the "carnal" Christian is simple. When self is allowed control of the life, that is sin and needs to be confessed as such. There may be other specific sins that need to be confessed. God has promised in 1 John 1:9 to *forgive* the sin and *cleanse* the sinner. Then simply ask God to take control.

Peace of mind and heart comes from knowing God, from believing that He makes no mistakes, and from allowing Him to be in control of the life. It is only through Jesus Christ that we can be freed from our guilt and feelings of failure.

"And the peace of God, which passeth all understanding, shall keep your hearts and minds through Christ Jesus" (Philippians 4:7, KJV).

Notes

[1] Betty Friedan, *The Feminine Mystique* (New York: Norton, 1963), p. 189.
[2] C. Sumner Wemp, *How on Earth Can I Be Spiritual?* (Nashville, New York: Nelson, 1978), p. 49.

Suggested Reading

James D. Mallory, Jr., *The Kink and I* (Wheaton, Ill.: Victor, 1973). A psychiatrist writes about how to take the "kinks" out of daily living. This book is humorous, human, and very helpful.

Josh McDowell, *More Than a Carpenter* (Wheaton, Ill.: Tyndale, 1977). For someone questioning the basic facts of Christianity and the reasons for the Christian's faith, this is a fine book.

Bruce Narramore and Bill Counts, *Guilt and Freedom* (Irving, Calif.: Harvest House, 1974). This book is a study of guilt and how to be freed from it. Excellent!

C. Sumner Wemp, *How on Earth Can I Be Spiritual?* (Nashville, New York: Nelson, 1978). This volume will tell you how to stop living an up-and-down Christian life.

Chapter Seven

For Better or Else

We are both waiting at Gate 24 for the flight to New York. There is no doubt about it. She is a career woman.

Dressed for success, she wears a soft gray suit with a burgundy scarf at her neck, accented by simple but elegant gold jewelry. She wears large-framed glasses that give her a look of authority. She carries an impressive, yet feminine, leather briefcase.

Immediately I feel intimidated. Reverting to the self-conscious little girl from Milroy, Indiana, I wonder if my slip is showing.

Most of the passengers already have their boarding passes, so we soon begin the march through the tunnel to board the aircraft.

I spot the career woman in the window seat under my number, already busily examining papers from her briefcase. My seat is on the aisle, and the seat between us is empty.

"Hello, there." She smiles warmly, and I feel better already.

It's not long before we're engaged in conversation. She tells me that she is a buyer for a large department store. She is divorced and has two daughters in high school.

"When our children were born," she says frankly, "I was determined that I would not go back to work. I wanted to be at home with those babies.

"But when the younger one was six months old," she continues, "my husband was changing jobs and taking a big cut in pay. We simply would not be able to make it on that salary, so I *had* to go back to work. I found a job as a secretary for a buyer, thinking that I would work six months and then go back and stay at home with the girls. When I left the baby at the sitter's I cried and cried.

"By the end of six months," she says softly, "I had changed. It had *done* something for me to be out with adults. I found that I no longer wanted to be home with the children, cleaning house and changing diapers. I was no longer contented to have my husband be the center of my life; I no longer intended to devote myself entirely to my children's upbringing."

As I listen to this woman's story, I am astonished to hear her saying the same things I've been hearing from other, less "together" women.

"Frankly," she continues, "my husband just couldn't cope with my change in attitude. He never supported my working in any way. As a matter of fact, the more I advanced in my work, the more he dragged his feet and complained. We were fighting all the time about housework, about money, about the girls."

I interrupt to ask if she has ever had an interest in spiritual matters.

"I guess you could say I'm in limbo right now. Because I'm divorced, the church I used to attend has excluded me. Sometimes I feel I'd like to go to church again, but the feeling passes. I'm very busy with my career, so I really don't have time for all that. Also I think that religion tends to put down women, to keep them subservient. I'm not interested in that kind of thinking.

"I have very little respect for the marriage institution. I used to think marriage was sacred. But when two people stay together and destroy each other, there's nothing sacred about that. I found it very disappointing. Among my friends, I haven't seen any good marriages. I can't name one really happy couple."

Does she think that women going to work has had an impact on marriages?

"Definitely. As a result of a woman working, she has realized that she doesn't have to put up with the jerk who treats her like a maid."

The New York skyline is suddenly in view out the airplane window. The Statue of Liberty looks tiny and lonely in the distant harbor. As I glance at the career woman, I no longer feel intimidated. All of her outward signs of "togetherness" camouflage a woman who, underneath it all, also seems tiny and lonely. Though she is considered highly successful in her work, her personal life is bankrupt. As we leave the airplane and go our separate ways, I think about the career woman and the question I should have asked her: *Was it worth it?*

Just because that career woman's marriage ended in divorce is no reason to believe that all two-career marriages are doomed. On the contrary, when biblical relationships are maintained, the wife's career can bring a new sense of sharing into the marriage. But there are pitfalls to be avoided.

Woman's Work Affects Marriage

The marriage relationship is definitely affected when the wife becomes a wage earner. That is not to say that all divorce is caused by working wives, or even that working wives cause divorce. But when the wife works, there are areas of special concerns involving her relationship with her husband.

The statistics are a little unnerving. The divorce rate has been rising steadily with the numbers of women working. There are, no doubt, many other factors to be considered. But it is a fact that when the wife earns enough money to support herself, she is no longer economically dependent on her husband. A woman today may be able to command a job with both prestige and money—both of which may threaten the husband.

Vassar economist Shirley Johnson has calculated the hazard of divorce: for each additional $1,000 a woman earns, the chance of divorce increases by 2 percent.[1] (At that rate, heaven help the marriage where the wife earns more than $50,000 a year.) It is a simple fact that the more money a woman earns, the less likely she is to be married. She either never marries in the first place, marries later, or else her marriage ends in divorce.

Dr. James Dobson believes that the most common cause of divorce is the "breathless life-style" that leaves husbands and wives exhausted, "too tired to talk to one another or pray together or take walks together or have sex together, or be in love together."

Dobson concludes, "Certainly, if there is one consequence of having both parents work, it's this phenomenon of routine panic which I've described."[2]

Whatever else is happening, two-job marriages are increasing. They appear in no way to be a passing fad. As inflation spirals, more wives will join their husbands in the work force, adding to more than 25 million couples who were working by the beginning of the 1980s.

Couples Need Help

More than ever before, with the pressures of both partners' working added to the normal stresses of a marriage relationship, couples need *help*. Marriage has never been easy, but when Mom goes to work the best marriage can flounder. To maintain a successful marriage it is essential that *God's principles* guide the relationship.

Marriage is the closest, most intimate of all human relationships. It has the potential to be the source of either great joy or tremendous unhappiness.

Marriage was established by God, way back in Eden.

> Then the LORD God said, "It is not good for the man to be alone; I will make him a helper suitable for him." . . . So the LORD God caused a deep sleep to fall upon the man; and he slept; then He took one of his ribs, and closed up the flesh at that place. And the LORD God fashioned into a woman the rib which he had taken from the man, and brought her to the man.
>
> The man said, "This is now bone of my bones and flesh of my flesh; she shall be called 'woman,' for she was taken out of man."
>
> For this reason a man will leave his father and mother and *be united to his wife, and they will become one flesh.* [Genesis 2:18, 21-24, emphasis mine]

No other human relationship is described as *two* people's becoming *one,* and it is that specialness of marriage that makes it so beautiful.

God made all the creation and said it was "good." But of loneliness He said it was "not good." Woman was created to be her husband's "helper" or "helpmeet." Properly understood, there is nothing degrading about that role. It simply shows that *neither* marriage partner is complete without the other.

What does it mean to be a helpmeet? Simply stated, it is a wife working *with* her husband, not *against* him. They share common goals and ambitions, and they cooperate with each other to get the job done.

Let's say they are in a rowboat, and they are side-by-side, working together to reach their destination. If one of them stops rowing, the boat will go around in circles. They must continue to work together to reach their destination. But if she gets out of their rowboat and gets into her own rowboat and starts rowing by herself, they are no longer a team. If they have the same goal, they may soon be in competition to see who arrives first. Because she is in her own rowboat, she is more likely to choose a new destination, one different from her husband's. So, she will go her way, and he will go his, until there is a wide gulf between them.

Assertiveness and Explosions

The problem can begin before the wife ever goes to work. If she feels a need or desire to work away from home but does not talk about it with her husband or pray about it, she is bound to become frustrated and feel resentment. What happens too many times is that the wife keeps her feelings inside herself, not being honest with God or her husband about the way she really feels. Then one day there is an explosion.

The scene:

Wife has been working at home all day trying to finish sewing an outfit she is making for her daughter. While she sews she watches a talk-show host interview a special guest, an author of a new book on women's assertiveness. As wife listens, she becomes convinced that she has allowed people, especially her husband, to take advantage of her. *All I've ever done,* she cries to herself, *is do things for other people. Nobody around here cares about me.* She decides that what she needs to do is go back to college and finish work on her degree. *Then,* she thinks, *maybe somebody will respect me.* She thinks and ponders and stews all day.

Enter Hubby at 6:00 P.M. He is thinking about a sale he failed to close and is worrying about the commission he will lose if he doesn't. He is *not* thinking about his wife's ambitions. She is not thinking about his problems. Before his hat has hit the rack, she announces in the most "assertive" voice she can muster:

"I've made a decision. I'm enrolling in college, and I'm going to become a stockbroker."

Now Hubby, no matter how supportive he might be in theory, will not be thrilled at her announcement. *Oh, brother!* he thinks. *What next?* He has not been prepared for this moment.

According to Morton and Marjorie Shaevitz,[3] psycho-
therapists who specialize in advising two-career couples, he
will probably respond defensively in one of three ways:
 • "You can change, but leave me out of it." Because he does
not want to be considered a male chauvinist, he tells her to go
ahead and enroll in school. But she'd better make sure she's at
home when the kids get home from school and that dinner is
ready on time.
 • "You can change, but what will happen to the children?"
Hubby uses guilt as a weapon to see that the normal household routine is not upset.
 • "What's the matter? Don't I make enough money for
you?" Hubby, unprepared for his wife's overdetermined show
of assertiveness, feels threatened. He feels fear and confusion. He doesn't think in terms of what her needs might be;
he sees the situation only as a reflection of what must be his
own inadequacy.
Husbands, in general, are poorly prepared to deal with
even the slightest change in the normal household routine
that occurs when the wife becomes employed or goes back to
school with the goal of becoming employed.
The Shaevitzes say there are six main problem areas:
1. *Issues of child care.* The wife feels "most guilty" and the
husband "most accusatory."
2. *Sharing the household responsibilities.* "Initially there
seems to be great confusion as to who should be doing what
and with whom."
3. *Money and finances.* The wife's beginning steps usually
drain the budget rather than "adding anything to it."
4. *Issues of power and competition.* What happens when
"the wife is fairly successful and begins to approach her husband in terms of earning power"? That may sound like a question dealing with money and finances, but actually it is an
issue of power and competition between marriage partners.
What if the wife earns more than her husband? Stated

another way, the question might be: Does a wife undermine
her husband's authority when she makes more money than he
does?

The Bible does, indeed, give the husband the financial
responsibility for the home. It goes on to say that if he does
not care for his family, he is worse than an infidel (1 Timothy
5:8).

It is important that the wife respect her husband's feelings.
A good husband feels responsible to support his family, and a
wife can hurt him far more than she realizes by saying things
like this:

"Well, I just don't know what we'd do without my
paycheck."

"We couldn't afford to live in this house if I didn't work."

"We were in debt something awful until I got a job."

A husband needs to be respected, and that includes re-
specting his role as *provider.* No matter how much money the
wife earns, her attitude must be one of giving honor and
respect to her husband.

A young woman named Leslie works as a consultant in
computer technology. She already earns more than her husband, who is a school teacher.

Leslie says, "My husband is a *great* teacher. He has so
much to give those kids, and he loves his work. He also is a
coach, and he really enjoys it. The problem is that he can't
make enough money as a teacher for us to live on. He is very
much in favor of my earning more than he does!"

It is the husband's responsibility to take care of the material
needs of the family. But it is entirely possible that when husband and wife both prayerfully seek God's perfect will for
their lives, they may come to the conclusion that their family's
needs could best be met by the wife's being the higher wage
earner.

We have to get back to the basics. Our purpose in life is to
bring glory to God through His plan for us and on His terms.

Neither husband nor wife should be working for his or her own glory. God's plan for us goes far beyond anything the human mind can comprehend; His goals for us are limited only by our refusal to let Him work through our lives.

In a marriage where both partners are seeking God's will in their lives and in their marriage, the question really is, What is God's best for our family? A husband who is committed to Jesus Christ and filled with the Spirit will not be jealous or resentful; he will rejoice with his wife that God is blessing them. A Spirit-filled wife will honor her husband and treat him with respect. The amount of money being earned by either partner is beside the point. If the two of them are *one*, what is the problem?

5. *Fears of outside sexual involvement.* Though the Shaevitzes call it "often a fantasy," there are clear dangers when a woman enters the world of men.

Gloria Norris and JoAnn Miller report in *The Working Mother's Complete Handbook* that "by the time employed wives reach their late thirties, they are more than *twice* as likely as housewives to have affairs!"[4]

One woman who has worked a number of years says she believes that many women get involved because they are naive. They don't realize that to some men flirting is a habit and sexual involvements mean *nothing*. A woman who has been home for years might meet this kind of character and think, *Oh, I had no idea I was so attractive.* Like a swooning teenager she might think, *He must be madly in love with me.*

It is a sad fact of life that husbands and wives see each other at their worst and see men and women in the business world at their best. One Christian woman who started working at a bank after being married for fifteen years saw a certain man at the bank daily. Every day he told her she looked pretty. She had not been told she looked pretty in fifteen years. She found that she took a little more time and effort with her makeup each morning and anticipated his greeting. It wasn't long before she was having an affair with the man.

Women who are housewives can and do have affairs if they choose to do so. Many women who work remain faithful to their husbands. But a woman does need to remember that dangers exist. She needs to know how to be friendly yet keep her distance with the men at work.

6. *Issues of primacy of careers.* Whose career is most important?

Traditionally it has been assumed that the husband's career is most important and that the wife's job would be relatively unimportant. That attitude was based primarily on economics; because he earned more money, his job was more important.

Changes are taking place. As affirmative action programs are implemented and mature, more couples are seeing the wife become the higher wage earner. Does that make her career more important than his? Her job may have more prestige than his. Does that make her job more important?

Janet is the private secretary for the legal counsel of a large, prominent firm. Her husband is an auto mechanic. He earns more money than she does, but her job is more prestigious. She is often included in social circles where her husband feels uncomfortable. What effect does that have on the marriage? It has the potential for *disaster* unless she continues to show respect for her husband.

One of the thorniest problems is the one of transfer. If either the husband or wife is offered a promotion that involves a transfer to another city, the offer can cause real problems as far as the other partner's career is concerned.

Some people's jobs are transportable; some are not. So it becomes an individual decision for each family to make, considering the good of the entire family.

That problem has the potential to break up families. One woman who has a very high-paying (but non-transferable) executive position is now married the third time because her first two husbands were offered promotions in another part of the country and she, both times, refused to go.

Another woman was with a large manufacturing firm and was offered a transfer with promotion. Her husband quit his management-level job to go with her but could not find another job on the same level in the new location. He suspected, but could not prove, that the new companies were afraid to hire him for fear that his wife would be transferred again.

Leslie, the computer consultant, has already discussed the possibility of transfer with her school-teacher husband. "He says that if I get a promotion, we'll go. His teaching area is industrial arts, and teachers are needed in this subject all over the country. But if my getting a transfer would hurt him in any way, I just would have to refuse it."

Competing or Completing

Phil and Myrna White know some of the hazards facing a marriage when both husband and wife work outside the home.

Phil and Myrna met while students at Moody Bible Institute. They began their marriage with dreams of serving the Lord with music, and they went on the road with a group of young singers and musicians in the Word of Life Ensemble, later called The New Creation. They traveled extensively in the United States, Canada, and South America.

Though their work was also a ministry, some serious problems emerged.

Myrna, with a clear and beautiful soprano voice, was lead singer; she was often in the spotlight in a literal sense. Phil, who did much of the arranging and background music for the group, was barely noticed.

"It began to gnaw at me," says Phil. "After the performances, people would crowd around Myrna, telling her how wonderful she was—while I was taking down the equipment."

Phil felt conflicting emotions and confusion about his "role."

"I grew up," he says, "in a Christian home. Somehow, from the Christian culture I adopted some assumptions that I discovered later to be false. One of those false assumptions was that the man of the family is *superior* to his wife. Here I was, married to a woman who was clearly my superior as far as singing and performing were concerned, and I felt that I was failing God in some way."

Phil and Myrna were facing one of the many problems and conflicts that confront working couples, but they were able to work out their difficulties in such a way that the Lord could be glorified.

Although Phil had a degree in music theory, he went back to school at Roosevelt University and took graduate courses in accounting, because he enjoyed math. He was not sure what he would do in the field of accounting, because he felt under pressure from others to continue in music. One of Phil's professors saw that he had ability in accounting and the potential to become a certified public accountant. That encouragement led to a complete change in career direction for Phil.

"Myrna also encouraged me," he says, "and I began to realize that I should be what God wanted me to be, not what others thought I should be. As I gained self-confidence, I was able to support Myrna wholeheartedly and encourage her to use the voice that God had given her." Once Phil became secure in himself and his abilities as a C.P.A., Myrna and her singing were no longer a threat to him.

Now Phil works as a C.P.A. for a retirement village, and he and Myrna work together in concerts. He arranges many of her songs and accompanies her on the twelve-string guitar. Because they are now the parents of three children, they limit their engagements to a certain number each month.

Phil and Myrna were able to come to grips with their problem because they were looking to Jesus Christ to show them the way. God showed them His will for their lives, and He will do the same for other working couples.

The Bible gives us a beautiful picture of marriage, of two people becoming one. The husband is to complement, or *complete*, the wife, and the wife is to complement, or *complete*, the husband.

Paul says in 1 Corinthians 7:3, "The husband should fulfill his marital duty to his wife, and likewise the wife to her husband," NIV. Though this verse is speaking about the sexual aspect of marriage, the most important "marital duty" is to *meet the needs* of the spouse, whatever those needs are.

Pastor Charles E. Perry, Jr., says, "We men just love to be complemented by our wives. We love our wives to meet our needs. When I was in seminary, my wife, Martha, worked hard to help me through school. She worked in an office all day and then typed papers for me all night. I really *appreciate* her hard work. Many men have had their wives help them like that, and they think it's *great*. But what if the wife believes the Lord is leading her to go back to school, to develop a skill, to use a talent? Is the husband willing to complement her? Will he pitch and in and help wash dishes and do laundry and sweep floors so that she can? Husbands and wives are to work together, encourage one another, and support each other."

More Valuable Than Rubies

Remember the virtuous woman of Proverbs 31? She worked both outside and inside the home, yet her relationship with her husband was not harmed. What did she do? If she were a working woman of the 1980s how would she protect her marriage?

• She gives her husband no reason to suspect her of any wrongdoing. He can totally *trust* her. "Her husband has full confidence in her" (v. 11, NIV).

• She is *for* him, not against him. "She brings him good, not harm, all the days of her life" (v. 12, NIV).

• She doesn't try to *upstage* her husband. He is honored in his own right. "Her husband is respected at the city gate, where he takes his seat among the elders of the land" (v. 23, NIV).
• She watches what she says, knowing the importance of speaking with *wisdom* and *kindness.* "She openeth her mouth with wisdom, and in her tongue is the law of kindness" (v. 26).
• The final test is the surest one. "Her children arise and call her blessed; her husband also, and he praises her" (v. 28) because she fears the Lord. "Charm is deceptive, and beauty is fleeting; but a woman who fears the LORD is to be praised" (v. 30, NIV).

Notes

[1] Shirley Johnson, as quoted by Caroline Bird in "Full-Time Homemaking Is Now Obsolete," a copyrighted interview in *U.S. News & World Report,* 9 July 1979, p. 47.
[2] James Dobson, "The Working Mother." Cassette. Educational Products Division, Word, Inc., Waco, TX 76703.
[3] Morton H. Shaevitz and Marjorie H. Shaevitz, "Changing Roles. Changing Relationships: Implications for the Mental Health Professional," *Psychiatric Annals,* February 1976, pp. 39-41. Used by permission.
[4] Gloria Norris and JoAnn Miller, *The Working Mother's Complete Handbook* (New York: Dutton, 1979), p. 217.

Suggested Reading

Gary Chapman, *Toward a Growing Marriage* (Chicago: Moody: 1979).
Darien B. Cooper, *You Can Be the Wife of a Happy Husband* (Wheaton, Ill.: Victor, 1975). This is an excellent book on marriage relationship.
Maxine Hancock, *Love, Honor & Be Free* (Chicago: Moody: 1975).
Tim LaHaye and Bev LaHaye, *The Act of Marriage* (Grand Rapids, Zondervan, 1976). The LaHayes give an honest and open discussion of the sexual aspects of marriage.

Chapter Eight

Mother Alone

Irene's eyes fill with tears as she talks.

"Do you know what it feels like to get fired? Well, I do. I got "fired" a year ago January when my husband came home and told me he'd filed for divorce.

"All of a sudden my world just caved in. I was no longer needed as a wife. Being experienced and dependable was not enough anymore. I had been replaced by a girl young enough to be his daughter, a swinger who feels comfortable in his bachelor pad, surrounded by girlie magazines.

"For seventeen years," she continues, "I'd wrapped my life around him and the kids. I was just a kid myself when we got married—I hadn't even finished high school. The only work I'd ever done was in the kitchen at the school cafeteria. The thought of going out into the business world terrified me.

"Two of our children are still at home, and I get thirty dollars a week for each of them for support. Have you ever tried to buy groceries for two teenage boys on sixty dollars a week? I'm just not making it. I can't pay my rent and utilities on what I make, let alone keep gas in the car. I just don't know what I'm going to do.

"The boys are basically pretty goods kids, but I find they are taking advantage of me more and more every day. Let's

face it, they are bigger than I am. If they want to do something, I can't stop them. They also seem to resent taking
instructions from me—a mere woman. They've picked up
some pretty chauvinistic attitudes.

"I'm going to have to find another place to live pretty soon,
because the people who own this house sold it. I just don't
know what to do, and I feel the weight of the world on my
shoulders."

Female-Headed Families

Irene is part of one of the fastest-growing phenomena in
American culture: the female-headed family. The number of
female-headed families is increasing almost ten times as fast as
the number of two-parent families. By the beginning of the
1980s, more than seven million women with more than nine
million children were living in families without fathers.
Though some of that single-parenting is the result of the
death of the husband, most cases are caused by divorce, sep-
aration, or a runaway parent.

A growing number of children are living with their fathers
after divorce, but usually it is the mother who is left with the
children. Money, for many, becomes the most pressing problem. Alimony is generally a thing of the past, and many
fathers ignore the court's order to pay child support. Some
fathers simply walk out the door and vanish, never to be heard
from again.

Veronica

Veronica had one child and was working on a management
level when her husband was transferred to Arizona.

"I was able to get a transfer, but it was a much lower position, both in pay and responsibility. My husband was traveling
all the time, and I never saw him. In the evenings and on
weekends, I became a very lonely housewife. I was living in a
big beautiful house, but my thrill of the week was getting my

TV Guide and circling the shows I wanted to watch. My daughter never even saw her father. Finally I said, 'I can't stand living this way.' So I called a mover and packed up our things and I came back home. That was the end of my marriage, such as it was.

"When I came back I got a job again with the same company, but I had to take a big step down from where I'd been before. My daughter and I moved into this tiny little apartment in a bad section of town—that was all I could afford. My first day back at work I went out to the car and it wouldn't start! I sat there and put my head down on the steering wheel and sobbed. The responsibility of everything was just overwhelming. Then all of a sudden I realized that my ex-husband didn't know a thing more about cars than I did. What would he do if the car wouldn't start? He'd call a garage. So that's what I did. After that I think I knew I'd be able to get along all right."

Veronica is learning to manage as a single parent though it is a struggle. "I guess I'm still trying to figure it all out."

Maureen

Maureen was fixing supper one evening when the doorbell rang. It was a policeman saying he was sorry to disturb her but she had better come with him to the hospital. Her husband had been on his way home when he went around a curve and was hit head-on by a drunk driver. In shock she went to the hospital, only to learn that he had been pronounced dead on arrival. With a preschooler and two children in elementary school, Maureen walked through the next days numbly. It was three months before she realized the finality of the situation.

"Financially," she says, "I didn't really have to get a job. And with three kids there was certainly enough to do. But, even with the kids, I was so *lonely*. I was going crazy in that house, knowing that George wouldn't be home tonight, not tomorrow night, not ever."

What Can I Do?

Whatever it is that causes a mother to be raising children alone and working at the same time, there are pressures and problems in coping with it all. Working and being two parents is a tough assignment.

Jenny is a woman whose husband left her several months ago. As a Christian, she agonized about the divorce.

"I can't separate my 'working mother' status from my divorce," she says. "I never worked more than a few part-time hours here and there. I never believed a mother should work. I stayed home with the kids when they were little. When they started to school, I made sure I was home when they got home at three o'clock.

"My husband was not a Christian, and my faith was a constant source of irritation to him. I prayed for him. I loved him. I didn't nag him. I accepted him as he was. But it was no use. He wanted out of the marriage, and he left me.

"Some of my Christian friends were wonderful and supportive. They said things like, 'We love you. God will work it out. We're praying for you.' Others have hurt me deeply. They would pounce on me really hard, telling me that I should refuse to divorce my husband. They were very harsh and judgmental, saying things like, 'You must have done something to fail him.' I'm sure I did. We all fail. But I didn't need that load of guilt dumped on me.

"I thank God for granting me peace in a very difficult situation. Without God's peace I could never have dealt with the blow to my self-esteem, the sense of failure, the feeling of rejection, the hurt, the humiliation. I found great comfort in 1 Corinthians 7:15: 'But if the unbelieving depart, let him depart. A brother or sister is not under bondage in such cases: but God has called us to peace' [KJV]. It broke my heart that he left me, but through that verse God gave me peace about it.

"Work, of course, is a big problem. My children are used to

my being there. They like me to be home when they get
home from school. But I *have* to work. The child-support is
barely enough for groceries. I've been working at different
things part time, but it takes a lot of hours to make enough
money to pay the bills.

"I'm struggling with the realization that I'm going to have
to support myself, to make enough money for me to live on. I
geared my whole life around being a wife and mother. The
working world is a cold reality, and it is a *jungle* out there. I'm
just praying that God will provide me with a job that meets
my needs.

"It astonishes me, still, the responsibility of being a parent
twenty-four hours a day. It's almost crushing. My kids are too
old for a sitter, yet I'm not yet able to leave them home alone.
So I don't go out in the evenings. I can't. They still need
transportation—to and from ball practice, to and from work,
to and from activities. Their father lives nearby, but he is all
wrapped up in his new girl friend, so I don't feel comfortable
asking his help. The few times I have asked him to take one of
the kids someplace, he said he would, then he forgot to do it.
He's very undependable, so I just can't ask him to help.

"I have learned, though, to accept help from other people.
At first I had too much pride to accept help from family and
friends, but now I know that we *need* help, and I'm very
grateful for it.

"I've also found how great kids can be. The divorce hit them
hard; they were and still are angry with their father. I try to
never say anything against him, because that does not help
anything. But I do try to communicate with them and include
them in what's happening. It's hard knowing what to say and
what not to say. I don't want to worry them. But I do feel they
have a right to know what's going on. It's just wonderful how
they have given me support and encouragement. When I'm
having a hard day they try to cheer me up, saying things like,
'It's OK, Mom. We'll make it.' "

You Are Not Alone

Remember that God, if you truly trust Him, will meet you at the point of your need. He cares about you and wants you to turn to Him. No matter how lonely you are, you are *not* alone. He wants you to trust Him. You need not bear these burdens if you will give them to the Lord to bear for you, "Casting all your care upon him; for he careth for you" (1 Peter 5:7, KJV).

With so much responsibility falling on your shoulders, you may feel that you are, in a sense, imprisoned by it. The apostle Paul actually was in prison when he wrote the book of Philippians, and this is what he had to say:

"Rejoice in the Lord always. I will say it again: Rejoice! Let your gentleness be evident to all. The Lord is near. Do not be anxious about anything, but in everything, by prayer and petition, with thanksgiving, present your requests to God. And the peace of God which transcends all understanding, will guard your hearts and your minds in Christ Jesus. . . .

"I have learned to be content whatever the circumstances. I know what it is to be in need, and I know what it is to have plenty. I have learned the secret of being content in any and every situation whether well fed or hungry, whether living in plenty or in want. I can do all things through him [Jesus Christ] who gives me strength" (Philippians 4:4-7, 11-13, NIV).

Chapter Nine

Who Does the Dishes?

Without a doubt, the thorniest problem for most mothers who work outside the home is the work that still needs to be done *inside* the home.

The woman who has been at home with children for several years will probably find that her adjustment in the area of housework will be the hardest transition of all.

Housework itself might be the cause of real conflict between you and your husband, between you and your children, and between you and your idea of how it "should" be.

Women who are compulsive cleaners and panicky perfectionists will, no doubt, have the toughest time accepting the fact that Getting Everything Done is an impossible dream.

One woman confided to me that since she had been working away from home, her house had "gone to pot." Most women expressed a high level of anxiety about their ability to manage both the house and her job. As one woman said, "It is not only hard to get everything done; it's impossible! *Something* has to give, and it's usually the housework."

After working all day, it is depressing to come home to a house with unmade beds, breakfast dishes all over the kitchen, and last night's mess strewed about the living room. Even with all of the laborsaving devices in our modern homes, we still need to dust, sweep, scour, scrub, sort, wipe, wash, iron, fold, shop, put away, cook, clean up, and mop. Somebody, at least once in a while, has to water plants, change filters, wash windows, clean out garages and storage places. Many houses need ovens cleaned and refrigerators defrosted. Closets have a way of accumulating things that are never worn or used. Most houses and apartments soon are filled with clutter that seems to be moved from place to place, never getting put away. Kid's rooms can become incredible dungeons entered only by the most fearless.

Women who have gone to work after being home with the children several years may be in for a surprise. Says Caroline Bird in *The Two Paycheck Marriage:*

> When a wife goes to work she discovers that some of what she has done for her family will never be missed. Easiest to skip are the tasks that don't show, like washing the top of the refrigerator, cleaning out closets or ironing sheets. All but two of one hundred working women queried on their housekeeping never picked up their children's rooms, and sixty-nine never gave their homes a spring cleaning. An astonishing thirty-four saw no reason to make the bed for a house that stood empty all day, so they made them up only when they changed the sheets. An equal number never did ironing. One boasted that she didn't even own an iron.[1]

Some women soon find that old standards of perfection cannot be maintained, and that is upsetting to them. They feel guilty that they can't do everything their mothers did. Other women could not care less about how the house looks (whether they have an outside job or not) and live in continual disorder and chaos.

Somehow a balance needs to be reached. Striving for perfection will make you nervous and irritable. You will probably not accept help from your husband and children because they don't do the job as excellently as you do. You will be frustrated and upset and make everyone around you miserable.

On the other hand, children pick up bad habits from their parents. If you allow the house to be a continual wreck, your children will be disorganized and unproductive. If your husband has higher neatness standards than you do, the house will no doubt be the source of much conflict.

Despite the glowing reports in many magazines about the sharing of household tasks by husband and wife and the new marriage agreements where the husband promises to "love, honor, and mop the floor," the vast majority of women are still the ones in charge of household duties.

Some changes for the better are being made in this area. More and more men are realizing that there is nothing intrinsically feminine about housework. After all, men in the service have to "police the area," thay have "latrine duty," and they work "KP." That work is just work that needs to be done. They might not like it, but they do it.

Why Doesn't My Husband Help?

If a husband was raised in a home where his mother worked and his father and the children participated in caring for the house, he will probably feel rather comfortable sharing the household chores. If he never saw his father do anything around the house and he never held a broom or a dustcloth, he will need to adjust. But he certainly can do the work, and most of the time he will if he understands the need.

Another problem, of course, is that when couples decide that the mother should stay home with the children while they are young, it is natural for her to do most of the housework, because she is home all day, anyway. He may help with some of the work, but, mostly, she takes care of it. He may not even realize what she does, making her, in turn, feel unappreciated and resentful. Then when she does go to work, he might resist having to start doing things he has never done before. He might feel that she is gaining an exciting new job and he is losing his leisurely evenings.

Sometimes a woman is resentful that her husband is not helping, yet she never communicates to him her needs. Glaring looks and sarcastic remarks do not help. He cannot read her mind. This is an area where honest, open, unemotional communication is needed. For example:

"Honey, it's really frustrating for me to have to spend one or two hours in the kitchen in the evening by myself fixing supper and cleaning up. If we could work together, we could get finished so much faster and we'd have more time to enjoy each other."

He might never have considered that. Most husbands will respond.

It is important that the wife show her appreciation. We are told, these days, that we shouldn't feel grateful when our husbands shoulder part of the household responsibility. That is ridiculous. Showing appreciation is simply good human relations and applying the Golden Rule. We like people to appreciate what we do; why shouldn't we appreciate someone else's efforts?

Mobilize the Troops

If you have the idea that doing the housework is your responsibility and yours alone, you are cheating your children. They need to learn how to keep a place in order, and you can't start too young.

You can, however, start too old. If you have been everybody's servant until you take a job when your kids are teenagers, be prepared for war! You will likely hear something like this: "What?! Do the dishes? *I knew it! I knew it! You go out and get a job and I have to do all of* your *crummy work!*"

Don't despair. Teenagers can be taught to help. But be advised that they will try to get out of it by every ploy they can think of: ignoring you, arguing with you, "none of my friends have to wash dishes," shoving junk under the bed, and so forth. If they know you are serious, though, they will come through.

Some tips:

• First of all, talk with your husband. You must be "of one mind," and you need his support in getting everyone involved.

• The family conference is a superimportant vehicle of communication. You and your husband need to sit down with the kids and talk over everything about your job. That should be done *before* any changes come into their lives, but it is better late than not at all. Kids can deal with almost anything as long as they are prepared for it.

• Establish a routine. Let the children know *specifically* what their daily and weekly jobs are. Some people have success with charts and gold stars. If they help you, by all means use them. Remember, it's not what you *expect* from your children, it's what you *inspect* that will get done. You or your husband must follow up and check the work.

• It bears repeating: Start young. If you are home with your children while they are young, you'll be able to do a great deal of teaching at a time when they are eager to learn. Teach from the beginning that part of the game is putting everything away.

• Make it *easy* for your children to put things away. Clear out closets and shelves of excess clothes and toys. Put in shelves for toys and books and make sure everything has *a place*. Put a tension rod in a child's closet on his level so he can hang up his own clothes. You can move the rod up as he grows taller. A clothes hamper in the room will make it easier for him to drop in his dirty clothes. It's a long way to the bathroom.

• One mother of two teenage girls gives them two days to get clothes put away. Anything left out longer belongs to Mom, and she keeps it for a week.

• Use a comforter instead of a bedspread. Even a toddler

can pull up a comforter. The bed will be much easier to make
and the wrinkles underneath won't show.

• Realize that your child is a child. Don't expect adult standards. It is not realistic to demand perfection.

• On the other hand, don't let him get by with a sloppy job.
If he shoves all the grunge under the bed when he's supposed
to have cleaned his room, insist that he come back and clean it
out.

• To get the supper dishes done, rotate the kids as helpers.
Write their names down on a calendar so there won't be any
argument about whose turn it is.

• Help your child get started. Often the prospect of a job is
overwhelming, but once started it's not so bad.

• Help your child learn to *finish* what he has started. If he
quits in the middle of a job, call him back to complete it.

• Messes made should be cleaned up by the mess maker. If
someone bakes a cake, cleanup is part of the job. Have these
as rules of the house: If you turn it on, turn it off. If you open
it, close it. If you get it out, put it away.

• Kids need to know what is involved in keeping a house
clean. They need to know *how* to clean a toilet and other
charming little tasks. Give them the benefit of practicing at
home.

• Remember that the end result of kids' helping out at
home is not simply to get the housework done. A parent's job
is to teach a child to be independent.

Should Kids Be Paid for Work?

Paying youngsters for work done around the house is con-
troversial. Some people say no—they are part of the ranch;
they eat and sleep here; they shouldn't be paid to do part of
the work. Others say yes—why not establish early the con-
nection between work and money?

This is an area where you have to be guided by your own

convictions. If you think children should not be paid, then don't do it.

You may want to compromise by having them do certain chores without pay and others with pay. For example, children can make their beds, pick up their rooms, and help with the dishes without pay. Special jobs, like mowing the grass or painting a fence, can be done for pay.

Weekly Cleaning

Besides daily straightening, some deeper cleaning needs to be done on a regular schedule.

If you can afford to hire someone to come in to clean thoroughly once a week (or even once every two weeks) by all means do so! And don't feel guilty about it, feeling that you should be able to handle it all. Paid help might be the very best way of getting the floors mopped and waxed, the bathrooms cleaned, the whole house dusted and vacuumed, and whatever else you need to have done regularly. Think of it as an investment in your peace of mind.

Washing and Ironing

• If you have a small family, you can probably do all the wash in one evening. Try throwing in the first load as you leave for work, then finish in the evening.

• If you have a bigger family, you may need to do one or two loads a day. For one week *count* the number of loads you do and mark down what kinds of loads they are: all white, wash and wear, towels, and so on. Divide by the number of days, and do that many loads each day. For example, if you do eight loads a week and want to wash only on Monday, Tuesday, Wednesday, and Thursday, then do two loads each of those days.

• Do you find yourself continually re-sorting laundry? Invest in hampers to keep in the laundry area. You may need five hampers, one for each type load: all white, jeans and sweatshirts, light gentle, dark gentle, and colored towels and sheets.

• Make sure each family member has his or her *own* towel rack and insist that they all hang up towels after showering. If you don't want to install more racks, you can buy a floor-to-ceiling pole with three or more racks. That effort will cut your towel washing in half.

• Buy a plastic dishpan for each family member. When you take clothes out of the dryer throw each person's things into his or her own tub (except for things that go on hangers). Each person is responsible to fold and put away his things and then return the dishpan to the laundry area.

• Eliminate the need to iron. Buy only wash-and-wear clothing and get rid of things that need ironing. If your husband needs to wear shirts that are starched and ironed, send them out to the laundry. Unless you are crazy about ironing, it is worth the expense.

Meal Planning and Grocery Shopping

You will save both time and money if you plan your meals for a week at a time and go to the grocery store only once a week.

What happens if you don't plan? The jingle runs through your head all the way home from work: "You deserve a break today," and off you go to the golden arches.

No matter what they say, eating out is not cheaper than eating at home, especially if you are feeding more than one or two people. Eating out can become a habit that takes a huge bite out of your paycheck. Families now spend 37 percent of every food dollar at restaurants, and industry experts anticipate that that figure will rise to 50 percent by 1990. One of the reasons for the increase is, of course, the fact that more and more women will be working.

The main reason we go out for food so often is poor planning. There is nothing wrong with going to a fast-food restaurant occasionally, and studies have shown that the food in some of them is quite nutritious, especially if lettuce and tomato are included. It's just that going out to eat often is without a doubt going to cost more in money and valuable family time at home together.

Here are some tips for planning and preparing the evening meal:

• Instead of wondering, "What should I fix for dinner tonight?" on the way home from work, plan the evening meals a week in advance. Efficiency experts have determined that most families have an average of twenty-two dinner meals that they like and have repeatedly. Take a minute to write out *your* list of family favorites. Try to come up with fourteen or twenty-one meals. That is enough for two or three weeks. You can either rotate the meals or choose the ones that strike your fancy.

• When you spend time cooking, *really* cook. Never cook just one meal at a time. Double or triple each recipe and freeze several meals. If you have enough freezer space, you can cook a big pot of chili; a double batch of spaghetti sauce with meatballs; and three chickens, which can be made up into casseroles or chicken and broth. If you cook all those meals at once, you'll save on energy (yours), and you only have to clean up one mess.

• For recipes calling for cubed, cooked chicken, cook several chickens at once. Remove the chicken from the broth, bone, and cut meat into chunks. Put 1½ to 2 cups of cubed chicken into each freezer container and cover with broth. Freeze until you need it. Use in casseroles, chicken and noodles, or chicken chow mein. If you want cubed chicken not covered with broth, just cube and freeze in plastic bags.

• When you buy celery and green pepper, take part of it and chop as you would for most recipes. Freeze in plastic bags. When you need it, it's ready. Just pour out the amount needed, then return the bag to the freezer. These work well for any cooked dish. Onions can also be chopped and frozen, but they do not saute as well as fresh.

• Prepare all your fresh salad ingredients right after grocery shopping. Invest in a large, plastic airtight container. Wash your lettuce and spinach and *dry thoroughly*. Those can go directly into the plastic container. Green pepper and tomatoes can be stored in this container, but they should be in separate plastic bags. Use old peanut butter jars (with the wide mouth) to have radishes, carrots, and celery cleaned and ready to use. Just fill the jars with cold water to cover the vegetables and seal tightly. Carrots and celery sticks can be stored together; radishes should be stored separately. Fresh vegetables in salads are wholesome foods that can be the most creative part of the meal. The secret is having the vegetables cleaned ahead of time so that it is *easy*. Vary the salad with toppers such as cheese, chopped egg, alfalfa sprouts, sunflower seeds, peanuts.

• Keep your freezer stocked with vegetables your family likes. Potatoes for baking and different kinds of rice can be quick and easy side dishes.

• Fresh fruit is the best dessert. Slice an orange in quarter-inch slices, then cut the circles in half to make orange "smiles." Apple wedges, bananas, pears, peaches—any kind of fresh fruit makes a dessert far superior to sugary sweets. Fresh fruits are also quicker to prepare.

• List the groceries you will need for an entire week, planning what cooking will be done that week. Make sure you have all the ingredients you need for your recipes. Jot down the main course of each evening meal, but *keep it simple*. If you try to get fancy you'll end up with stuffed mushrooms and artichoke hearts, which the kids won't eat anyway.

• Some men love to do grocery shopping. Your husband might enjoy taking over that job. Half of shopping, of course, is the planning, and he might enjoy that, too. If you have a teenager who is old enough to drive, it would be a good learning experience to take over the jobs of planning and shopping. In some towns and cities there are grocery stores that make home deliveries or large order-by-computer services that do the grocery shopping for you. Investigate those services and use them if it makes sense for you.

Other-Than-Grocery Shopping

Shopping for things other than groceries can be a problem simply because of the time needed to do it.

Some women find that the mail-order catalogue is the fastest and easiest way to shop for everything from school clothes to curtains to hardware. Others find that their children really need to try on clothes to make certain they fit right. Both time and money will be saved by using a list to protect yourself from impulse buying.

"It was amazing when I went to work," one woman told me, "how much less money I spent. Finally I realized that I was spending less time browsing in the stores, buying things I didn't really need."

Try to make a once-a-month trip to the discount store to buy personal and household products. Some things are much cheaper than at the grocery, others are not. You just have to compare.

The Case Against Clutter

Your best efforts at keeping a house in order will be destroyed by clutter. Do you find yourself overwhelmed by odds and ends that seem to take over a house—books, magazines, mail, and just plain junk? A perfectly clean house will look a mess if there is clutter all around, and a house that is not so clean won't look bad if there is no clutter.

Get Rid of It!

Try to sort through one drawer or section of a closet each day, spending *no more* than fifteen minutes each day. If you try to do more you will have such a mess that you will wish you hadn't started! Have two boxes handy—one for trash and one for treasure.

Into the trash box put the things *nobody* would want: worn-out clothes, puzzles with missing pieces, toys broken beyond repair, and the like.

Into the treasure box put the still-good things you or your family members have not worn or used in the last year. They don't fit right, they don't look very good, or you have other things you like better. You may need to discard knickknacks you like, because you have just too many of them.

Throw the trash away. Put the treasure into a large garbage bag that can be taken to your favorite charity. You can, if you want to invest the time, have a garage sale. Whatever you do, get rid of it.

Realize that disposing of clutter is a continuing process. By the time you get through the house it will be time to start over again. Make a habit of passing along things to people who need them more than you do.

Make a place for everything in your home and *try* to keep everything in its place. If there is no special place to put something, it gets left out or it gets put into a drawer so you can never find it again.

Paper Jungle

Stephanie Winston in *Getting Organized* suggests that to sort out paper clutter you need (1) a waste basket and (2) four file folders marked (a) Things to Do, (b) To File, (c) Your Spouse's Name (if you have one), and (d) Financial.[2] (You might want to add one file folder for each member of your household who receives mail.)

The secret to getting paper clutter under control is to make a decision regarding each piece of paper as it comes into your hands, and then put it into the wastebasket or one of the files.

Take about one hour each week to file, pay bills, and make
sure the "Things to Do" are done.

Magazines and newspapers need to be scanned and articles
clipped if you think you might refer to them in the future. If
you find that you aren't reading the periodicals that you are
taking, drop the subscriptions. It's a waste of money and space
to pile up unread magazines.

Before Leaving the House

If you can do just four things before you leave the house
each morning, it will be so much nicer for you to come back to
in the evening:

• Go through each room with a trash bag, picking up all
trash, newpapers, and so forth. Also take a basket and put into
it everything that needs to be put away in another room. Put
the basket in a closet.

• Rinse and stack dishes. Put them in the dishwasher if you
have one. Wipe off table and counter.

• Clear off bathroom counters and wipe quickly.

• Have everyone make his or her own bed. Only persons
who sleep in baby cribs are exempt.

If those four things can get done in the mornings, you will
have a much better day.

One couple found that their mornings were simply too hec-
tic to get those things done, yet it upset them to come home
to a messy house. They decided it was worth the expense to
hire a neighborhood high-school girl to "whip the house into
shape" after school. They paid her a few dollars a day and
were delighted with the arrangement.

Sharing the Load

As more and more women enter the work force, more and
more households will be facing a housework crisis. But as all of
the members of the family participate in the work, they will
begin to realize the blessings to be found in bearing one

another's burdens and sharing one another's loads.

It takes physical and emotional strength to work all day and then face more work at home. Remember that the Lord promises to give His children strength when they need it:

He gives strength to the weary,
And to him who lacks might He increases power.

. . . .

Yet those who wait for the Lord
Will gain new strength;
They will mount up with wings like eagles,
They will run and not get tired,
They will walk and not become weary.

Isaiah 40:29, 31 (emphasis mine)

Notes

[1] Caroline Bird, *The Two-Paycheck Marriage* (New York: Rawson, Wade, 1979), p. 92.

[2] Stephanie Winston, *Getting Organized* (New York: Warner, 1978), p. 68.

Suggested Reading

Stephanie Winston, *Getting Organized* (New York: Warner, 1978). This book is loaded with information on organizing your life. Its ideas for organizing the home are especially helpful.

Shirley Convan, *Superwoman* (New York: Bantam, 1978). This volume contains a hodgepodge of information about everything from spot removal to making your own cleaning solutions.

Chapter Ten

Money Matters

When Mary Alice arrived at work that first Friday morning, her heart did a little dance as she saw what was waiting for her. Her first paycheck! She hoped nobody noticed that she was trembling. *How silly can you get,* she thought. *It's only money!*

When she pulled the paycheck out of the envelope, she was horrified at the small amount. Taxes and Social Security took a *chunk.*

Still, it was nice to be *paid* for working.

Money is not the only reason for working, but it is the most compelling one. Many women work because they are the sole supporters of their families. Other women work to help their husbands meet the rising costs of raising a family. Some women have no financial need to work, but they find it personally gratifying. There are even women who lose money working, because their expenses exceed their incomes, but generally that loss is considered an investment in future potential as a wage earner.

In a recent survey conducted by *Redbook,* more than half the women who responded to the poll said their families "would find it impossible to get along without their earnings." But four out of ten said "the money they earn is less important

117

than the 'pleasure' or 'fulfillment' or 'recognition' they get from working."[1]

As I talked with a number of mothers about the "why" of their working, most of their reasons involved money.

Elaine: (She and husband Matthew have a three-year-old daughter.) "Matthew does not like my working. As soon as it's financially feasible I want to stay home. I want another baby, but not until I can stay home. It's bad enough making arrangements for one! But Matthew is still in the process of getting set up in his own business. We need the money."

Becky: (She is the mother of two preschoolers.) "I went back to work when my husband changed to a sales job. He was going to be working on commission, and the potential was good. I didn't know until later that on the aptitude test they gave him, he figured out what they wanted him to say. He answered the way an outgoing, gregarious salesman would answer. He never sold a thing. I *had* to work, if we wanted food on the table.

Marie: My husband left me for a younger woman. I suddenly found myself with two children to raise and not nearly enough money to live. When my ex-husband remarried he lost interest in our kids and stopped paying support. It's been a constant battle."

Economic Need

"Economic need" can have many shades of meaning. The woman may be the sole supporter of the family and as such does not have the luxury of *choosing* to work. She has no choice.

Because of dizzying inflation rates, over a million women in this country are "moonlighting," holding down *more than* one job.

Consider the divorced mother of two children in Atlanta, who manages to work three jobs. *U.S. News and World Report* reports that she works full time for the government and has two part-time jobs—selling dinnerware and doing work for a booking firm.

She says, "It's not because I want to that I work at three jobs, it's because I have to. It is the result of continuous inflation—the rise in groceries, rent, gas, doctor bills for growing children and their entertainment, everything."[2]

Inflation and the high cost of raising children often drive mothers to work when many of them would rather stay at home.

"Economic need" may mean other things. She may want a second car or new living room furniture. She may want to earn enough money to pay the orthodonist or the additional cost of a private school.

Another mother might go to work to pay debts incurred by unwise credit buying.

We live in a materialistic society, constantly under pressure for more *things*. Hoffman and Nye in *Working Mothers* say, "American advertising has succeeded in keeping desires for material goods beyond the ability of people to obtain them."[3]

Many women go to work to maintain a standard of living that has suffered because of inflation or the loss of family income; others enter the job force to improve the family's life-style. The two-income family has brought a phenomenally high standard of living to record numbers of working-class families.

Many professional people with awesome combined incomes, while grappling with income tax brackets, live in what *U.S. News and World Report* calls an "uneasy affluence" with a "buy now, pay later" philosophy.

Buying things such as airplanes and expensive ski equipment, they have no trouble living just beyond their means. "The catch is that the good life could evaporate fast if one of the partners were to leave the work force."[4]

Overspending

In spite of the addition of a second income to many households, in many cases that has done little to relieve the basic financial problem: overspending.

If you doubt that overspending is a problem, just consider this. In 1978 the average family earned $14,100. The average family *spent* $15,400.00. That is $1,300 of debt, which tends to accumulate, building and building year after year until the family "suddenly" finds itself in a financial bind.

Sometimes a mother goes to work to ease the financial pressure caused by overspending. Larry Burkett, founder of Christian Financial Concepts, a counseling organization in Norcross, Georgia, says, "Many times when the wife goes to work in a situation where the problem is over-spending, it's like putting a Band-Aid on the symptom. The real problem is lack of discipline. Her money won't help at all unless they *discipline* their spending. What they usually will do is keep on overspending at a higher level."[5]

Feeling Affluent

Many times a woman will jump into a working situation and dramatically change her and her family's life-style. At first she is usually euphoric with her newly discovered financial power and the personal freedom promised by it. The husband also may sense a feeling of relief to have someone sharing the financial load. They begin to *feel* more affluent, and they "reward" their hard work by frequently eating out and taking trips. Family bankruptcies often are *caused* by an increase in income. Because creditors now by law must grant credit to women (which is certainly the way it should be), couples sometimes go a little crazy with their borrowing power. Soon they have moved into a bigger house with a bigger mortgage at a higher interest rate. They now have two big car payments, stretched out over four years. They don't think about the fact that cars depreciate so fast that after the first year or so they generally are worth less than the remaining payments. To their horror, they discover that even with two incomes they are still overspending. Their expenses have mounted to the place that even if the wife hates working, she can't quit.

Once Again, Communication

You must take the time to sit down and figure where you are, where you are going, and where your money should be going. Most families have *no* plan. They make the big payments, then spend the rest until it is gone. If there's too much month at the end of the paycheck, they use the automatic check loan or make purchases with Visa to make up the difference. All of a sudden, here comes Christmas and the washing machine breaks down, and there is real trouble with pyramiding debt.

If you are married, you and your husband *must* work out this problem together. You can't do it alone, and he can't do it alone. The two of you, working together, are the only ones who can get yourselves off this treadmill. It may be hard to talk about it, because money and power are so closely tied together, and someone may feel threatened.

Who takes care of the financial books in your family? It should be the person who is better at detail work. A person who is frustrated by detail work will soon have things in such a mess that nobody will be able to figure them out. You and your husband need to establish a regular, scheduled time to communicate with each other about your money. Write it down on your calendar. Most couples never *talk* about money; they just *fight* about it. It is estimated that 80 percent of the divorces in this country started with financial troubles.

One of you may tend to be a compulsive spender, using spending to somehow give you a "lift." Remember Blondie in the cartoons? Whenever she and Dagwood had a fight, she would buy a new hat. Women are usually stereotyped as the compulsive spenders, but just as often it is men. Sadly, instead of buying hats, they buy *cars.*

If you have a tendency to spend impulsively, pray for God's help in dealing with that area in your life. He will help you if you want to be helped. But the most important thing to do is admit it. Recognize the tendency and be honest with yourself and with God.

To begin with, you need a simple analysis of where your money has been going. (This is not a budget.) Write out your major regular expenses (rent or mortgage payment, car payment, food, and utilities—don't forget insurance premiums, which may come due only once a year).

You may not know where the rest of your money is going, so for thirty days, you and your husband need to write down every *cent* you spend. That spending will include gasoline, lunches, medical and dental expenses, car upkeep, commuter fares, school lunches for children, clothes and shoes, dry cleaning, shoe repair, and so on. That is the only way you will be able to determine how you are spending your money.

Once you have those figures, you can start working on a budget. We haven't the space in this book to go into detail explaining how to set up a budget, but at the end of this chapter will be listed some materials to help you.

In the meantime, you can get started by making some evaluations.

• *Do you really need credit cards?* It's a fact that spending will be reduced at least 25 percent if you go "cash and carry." If you can't pay cash for it, do you really *need* it? What will happen if you don't get it?

• *What does it cost to work?* Working brings in money, but it also costs money. You need to sit down and write out all the costs involved with both of your jobs. Your costs depend on the kind of work that is being done. People who are self-employed also have to think of all the costs involved in running a business. Transportation and child care are the most obvious expenses, but there are many others. Clothing itself, plus dry cleaning and laundry, can be expensive. Where do you eat lunch, and how much does it cost? What about house-cleaning help?

• *Get on monthly billings.* Wherever possible, especially with automobile and home insurance, try to get on a monthly payment plan. Many companies offer that service at a very reasonable rate, and it will help balance your spending over the year. Also, utilities can usually be paid on a monthly plan. That will help simplify your budgeting.

• *Study your transportation expenses and needs.* How much of your income is spent on car payments, upkeep, gasoline, and parking? Is there a better way? Can you use a car pool? Can you ride public transportation? Can you live closer to work or work closer to home?

• *Look at your housing and car payments.* Houses and cars are budget wreckers. Larry Burkett says that in 1978 consumer debt rose 60 percent above the previous year, partly because so many families thought they had to hurry and get into a house before the prices and interest rates climbed any higher.[6] The result, unfortunately, is that many families are strapped with a house payment demanding half their spend-able income, and there is simply not enough left for their other basic needs. Getting into less expensive housing is for many the only solution. You may be paying far more for your car than is reasonable, also. Those evaluations need to be made objectively and unemotionally.

Things cannot make us happy, but they can make us miserable if they are taking too much of our income to pay for them.

Jesus said, "Be on your guard against every form of greed; for not even when one has an abundance does his life consist of his possessions" (Luke 12:15).

• *We are God's stewards.* It may come as a surprise to you, but God is very interested in the way we manage our money. Don't believe that your job is the source of your money. Everything we have—our money, our time, our personal resources—are blessings from God. Stewardship is more than giving money to the church each week, though we certainly should support God's work financially.

A steward is someone who takes care of someone else's property. We are God's stewards, and we need to realize that *everything* we have is His.

Then we need to make a decision to give a portion of our earnings back to God in a regular, systematic way. That can only be done by deciding *ahead of time* that this "bill" will be paid first.

> Honor the LORD from your wealth,
> And from the first of all your produce;
> So your barns will be filled
> with plenty,
> And your vats will overflow with new wine.
> Proverbs 3:9-10

• *Save a penny.* Another decision needs to be made ahead of time, and that is to begin a *regular* savings plan. The most convenient way to save is through a payroll savings plan. An amount that you determine in advance is deducted from your pay before you get your check. Because you don't see it, you won't miss it.

> In the house of the wise are stores of
> choice food and oil,
> but a foolish man devours all he has.
> Proverbs 21:20, NIV

• *Are there more headaches in April?* Seek an expert to help you with the tax problems that arise when family income is increased. Look at investments designed to help that situation. Tax-free municipal bonds and tax-deferred annuities are possibilities. Tax forms have become so complicated that it is probably well worth the expense to hire a competent accountant to take care of your taxes for you.

The Scriptural principle is this: "Render to Caesar the things that are Caesar's" (Luke 20:25). We are to be scrupulously honest in figuring our taxes, claiming deductions, and every other aspect of dealing with taxes. At the same time, we need not pay *more* than we are required to pay. Good counsel can help us figure the correct amount—no more and no less.

"For because of this you also pay taxes, for rulers are servants of God, devoting themselves to this very thing. Render to all what is due them; tax to whom tax is due; custom to whom custom; fear to whom fear; honor to whom honor" (Romans 13:6-7).

• *Where to invest?* Investments must be made with wisdom and prudence. Larry Burkett offers these guiding principles:

1. Stick with what you know.
2. Don't use borrowed money.
3. Buy assets with utility value.
4. Seek competent counsel.
5. Wait on God.[7]

> He who works his land will have
> abundant food,
> but the one who *chases fantasies*
> will have his fill of poverty
>   Proverbs 28:19, NIV, emphasis mine

His or Hers?

The way a couple handles income depends to some extent on their plans for having more children. If another baby is a possibility, the couple should not presume to commit the wife's earnings to living expenses. They can save it for one-time purchases or a down payment, but they must not include it as a means for paying for recurring expenses. Otherwise they will *have* to have her income.

Other than that situation, it is best to put all income together and not separate it according to "his" or "hers." In marriage, two are to become one, and that includes the area of money.

Unpredictable Income

If you are going into a business where you will be self-employed, or if you are in sales or another job with unpredictable or fluctuating income, here is some more advice from Larry Burkett.

During the first year:

• Establish a stringent budget for business expenses. Know *exactly* how much you are spending and don't go over the budget you have allowed. If you don't control your spending, you will be spending more than you earn, putting even more stress on your husband's earnings.

• *Anticipate* taxes. If you are self-employed, all the money you bring in is *not* spendable. You probably are used to seeing your husband's paycheck after the taxes are taken out. If you are self-employed you must *plan* for taxes. Fill out a quarterly tax return.

After you have been in business for a year or more, you can work up a budget based on last year's income and divide by twelve. Take a very *conservative* approach.[8]

Trouble?

If you are facing financial problems, remember that you didn't get into debt overnight and it will take a while to get out. You need to seek competent financial counseling.

Here are three places you can go:

• Contact your pastor and request financial counseling. It may be that he or one of the laymen of the church have had training in financial management. Christian Financial Concepts is in the process of training five thousand nonprofessionals across the country to minister in that area.

• Go to the Consumer Credit Counseling Service, a nationwide, nonprofit organization.

• Perhaps you know and trust an accountant or other financial adviser in your community to whom you could go.

What, Me Worry?

You may not be having real financial problems at this point, but you do feel the need to become more disciplined about money. The Bible tells us we are not to *worry* about money but we are to *plan* the way we use it (see Matthew 6:27-34).

"For which one of you, when he wants to build a tower, does not first sit down and calculate the cost, to see if he has enough to complete it? Otherwise, when he has laid a foundation, and is not able to finish, all who observe it will begin to ridicule him, saying, 'This man began to build and was not able to finish'" (Luke 14:28-30).

Notes

1 Morton Hunt, "Making a Living Versus Making a Home," *Redbook*, April 1978, p. 70.
2 "How Families Try to Outwit Inflation," *U.S. News & World Report*, 23 April 1979, p. 29.
3 Lois Wladis Hoffman and F. Ivan Nye, *Working Mothers* (San Francisco: Jossey-Bass, 1974), p. 41.
4 "Two Incomes: No Sure Hedge Against Inflation," *U.S. News & World Report*, 9 July 1979, p. 45.
5 Larry Burkett, in a telephone interview with Mary Beth Moster, Spring 1980.
6 Ibid.
7 Larry Burkett, *Christian Financial Concepts*. Study guide for cassette series by that name. Christian Financial Concepts, 290-A Norcross-Tucker Road, Norcross, Georgia 30071.
8 Burket telephone interview, Spring 1980.

Suggested Materials

Larry Burkett, *Your Finances in Changing Times* (San Bernardino, Calif.: Campus Crusade for Christ, 1975).
Larry Burkett and Horace Holley, *Family Financial Planning*

Workbook (San Bernardino, Calif.: Campus Crusade for Christ, 1979).

Larry Burkett, "Christian Financial Concepts," Christian Financial Concepts, 290-A Norcross-Tucker Road, Norcross, Georgia 30071. Six tapes with workbook.

For additional information, write to Christian Financial Concepts at the above address.

Chapter Eleven

A Time for Everything

Evelyn Yoder looks nervously into the rearview mirror, intently watching for a highway patrolman as she crushes the accelerator to the floor. It's the second day this week she's been late for work.

She tries to fix her hair as she drives, but it's impossible. *What a mess*, she thinks with contempt.

She arrives at the office breathless, disheveled, a far cry from the poised and confident working women on the magazine covers.

Evelyn has forgotten what it was like to be relaxed. There is always so much to do—too much to do and not enough time to do it.

She thinks about the clutter all over the house, the unmade beds, and the breakfast cereal sticking to the bowls left on the table. Suddenly she remembers that today was the day son Alex was supposed to take Kool-Aid for the class party, and she had forgotten to send it.

Her desk at work is covered with papers to be sorted through and filed. Everytime she is able to start sifting through it, another more urgent assignment lands on her desk.

129

I can't seem to get my act together, she groans inwardly, convinced she must be the only woman in America who is "swamped" so much of the time.

Cheer up, Evelyn. You have lots of company. Part of the reason you feel so frustrated is that you really *do* have a lot to do. But there *is* a better way of doing it.

Getting Your Act Together

The hardest job for the working mother is Getting Everything Done. Her job, her husband, the kids, the house, shopping, cooking, cleaning, the laundry—all of that takes *time,* and there is never enough of it.

In this chapter we're going to talk about how we can better *manage* our time.

Before we even begin, however, we need to realize that no matter how well organized and well ordered a person's life is, there will always be things that will go wrong. *Planning* is the key to minimizing the chaos. The busier we are, the more we need to plan. But remember Murphy's Law: "If anything can go wrong, it probably will."

Even with the best planning, things will go amiss, and we have to adjust, rethink, and try again. But the better we plan, the better we're able to meet the unexpected.

In *Strategy for Leadership,* Edward Dayton and Ted Engstrom say, "Although we have learned that we live in an imperfect world, the unexpected or unpredictable keeps throwing us off balance. With planning, we attempt to wipe away some of the mist from the window of the future and reduce the number and impact of surprises."[1]

It all begins with our attitude toward time.

Time is precious. Often it is more valuable than money. Each of us has twenty-four hours every day to spend whether we want to or not. How we use those hours reveals our values, our purposes, and our goals. We *make* time for the things that are important to us.

"So teach us to number our days, that we may apply our hearts unto wisdom" (Psalm 90:12, KJV).

It is possible, of course, to overschedule and overplan; making an inflexible, straitjacketed schedule that has the potential to make you its slave. That is *not* what we need! We must be flexible; nobody needs flexibility more than a mother.

But we do need a system.

Managing Ourselves

In *The Making of a Christian Leader*, Ted Engstrom says, "In the final analysis, managing our time really means managing ourselves. We have to budget our time just as carefully as we have to budget our money." He goes on to say, "How often we hear, 'I wish I knew how to manage my time better.' Rarely do we hear, 'I wish I knew how to manage myself better.' But that's really what it comes down to."[2]

What's Really Important?

A distinction must be made between that which is *urgent* and that which is *important*. It was Dwight D. Eisenhower who said, "The important is seldom urgent, and the urgent is seldom important."

Most of us hurry and scurry, feeling harried and rushed. We snap at our kids and kick the cat. We feel like we are in a pressure cooker and can't get out.

We need to remember that Jesus never appeared in a frantic hurry. He didn't say, "Oh, I'm late. I'm late. There's a whole bunch of people over in Capernaum who are sick. Somebody's got to heal them." No, He was calm because He knew that He was doing the Father's will. He didn't heal *everyone*. He didn't convince everyone to believe in Him. He just did what He was supposed to do.

The difference is that He knew exactly what the Father's purpose was in His life on earth. He knew His assignment. His mission was to (1) live a perfect life, (2) die for our sins, and (3) leave behind disciples to pass along the wonderful news about Him to others and, ultimately, to future generations.

Studying the Bible is *important*, but other things can seem more urgent. Developing our God-given talent is *important*, but it is not urgent. Taking the time to communicate with husband and children is *important*, but it rarely seems urgent unless there is a crisis. How many times do those important things get shoved aside by the urgent things?

Priorities

Before we can even begin to look at techniques for time management, we must establish our priorities. The secular world with its "do your own thing" philosophy has almost removed any sense of need for settling in our own minds what is really important. In today's world, looking out for "number one" has top priority, but many men and women who have tried living by that philosophy have found it an empty, unsatisfying way to live.

The Bible gives us some guidance in the establishing of priorities. Some of us may find it against our nature to accept those teachings of Scripture, but God gives us that guidance for *our own benefit*. Much of the stress and strife in our lives is caused by the conflict produced when our lives are out of a divinely-ordained balance. That something has priority does not mean that you will devote more hours each day to it. It does mean that it is *set above* other things.

Here is a simple listing of biblical priorities:
1. God
2. Family
3. Work

Priority Number One: God

"But seek ye first the kingdom of God, and His righteousness" (Matthew 6:33, KJV). God must come first. We must give Him first place and live as He wants us to live.

Are you worried about paying the rent, buying the groceries, getting that certain shiny red bicycle for Christmas? It is in the context of worrying about things like those that Jesus tells us to seek *first* the kingdom of God:

"Do not be anxious then, saying, 'What shall we eat?' or 'What shall we drink?' or 'With what shall we clothe ourselves?' For all these things the Gentiles eagerly seek; for your heavenly Father knows that you need all these things. *But seek first His kingdom and His righteousness; and all these things shall be added to you* (Matthew 6:31-33, emphasis mine).

Spend time every day with our heavenly Father. Get to know Him. You can't really trust a person unless you know that person. An excellent series of booklets that help in beginning Bible study is *Ten Basic Steps to Christian Maturity* (Campus Crusade for Christ, Arrowhead Springs, San Bernardino, CA 92403). Even if you can answer only one or two questions each day, that will be of great benefit to you.

The story of Mary and Martha illustrates the importance of true worship. Mary "sat at Jesus' feet, and heard his word," while Martha was "cumbered about much serving" (see Luke 10:38-42). Jesus gently rebuked Martha because she gave her *work* a higher priority than Himself.

Set aside time each day to talk to God (prayer) and have Him talk to you (reading His Word). The best time for you may be early morning; it may be on your lunch break. Whenever it is, write it down on your "To Do" list until it becomes a daily habit.

Priority Number Two: Family

The family is ordained by God, and our family relationships are second only to our relationship with God.

Within the family, the husband-wife relationship must have a higher priority than the parent-child relationship. Why is this so? The child will be *hurt* if the husband-wife relationship is not sound, and the husband and wife still have many years to spend together after the children are gone.

In real life, however, most often it is the husband-wife relationship that suffers when both partners work. Women will refuse to take time from the children, but as one woman says, "There's just not enough time for everything, so I take the time from the people who can take it—my husband and me." Though there are times when you must take time from your husband to attend the needs of your children, you must not neglect your relationship with your husband.

Our children, of course, are given parents for a purpose. Children are "loaned" to parents for about twenty years during which time the children should learn to make good choices, to make sound decisions, and to be able to live independently of parents. It is a project that requires years of training, discipline, and determination. One of our problems is that we become so busy with the *daily* that the twenty years are suddenly gone.

God's instructions to parents are simple, but what a challenge!

"Train up a child in the way he should go, even when he is old he will not depart from it" (Proverbs 22:6).

Besides our immediate household, we must not forget our larger "family," close relatives and other friends. Simply stated, this is caring for the needs of *others*. Many mothers feel grieved at how little time they have to spend with friends and relatives.

It is especially important for us to maintain contact with our women friends. So often when we go to work we never have time anymore for friends. It may be impossible to get together for coffee (as in the preworking days), but you might be able to work out an occasional lunch together. Who is that special friend of yours? Why don't you drop her a note today?

Another important person who must not be neglected is *you.*

The person who is most often neglected by the working mother is the working mother herself. When she does spend time doing something she really likes to do or something just for herself, she might even feel guilty.

You are very important. God created you, He loves you, and He even cared enough about you to become a Man and die for you.

Our bodies are tremendously important. If we are trying to manage our homes as well as a job, we must respect the needs of our bodies. Taking care of our bodies includes several areas: the proper foods, exercise, rest, and moderate living.

You must take care of yourself.

Priority Number Three: Work

The area that actually consumes most of our waking hours comes third on our list of priorities. We have much work to do—work on the job, work at home, and work for the Lord. We need to organize our lives so that we'll have time to do our work well and still not neglect God or our families.

Because most jobs are structured and you *have* to arrive and leave at a certain time, the work that is usually neglected is work at home and work for the Lord.

Work for the Lord is easily neglected, but it can be part of a busy person's schedule. God has given each of His children a gift that can be used in serving Him. We don't all have the same gifts, so our work will differ. Perhaps teaching a Sunday school class is a way you could serve the Lord, or you could sing in the church choir, or work in the nursery. If you work for a Christian organization, your work for the Lord is combined with your job, but there should still be time to serve in some area on a volunteer basis.

To work effectively for the Lord it is important to become established in a local church. You might use the excuse, "Well,

Sunday is our only day to sleep in," but that *is* just an excuse.
If something really is important to you, you can do it. Going
or not going to church is a *habit*, and you have the responsibility to develop that habit. Church is important both as a place
to *worship* (which has top priority) and as a place to *work*.

Be choosy about your church. Look for these things:
- Is it Christ-centered?
- Is it Bible-believing?
- Is there opportunity for fellowship with other couples in
your age group?
- Does it teach that salvation comes by knowing Jesus
Christ personally?
- Does it send out missionaries to reach others for Jesus
Christ?

Becoming active in the local body of believers is essential,
both to your continuing growth as a Christian and to your
relationships with others. The spirit must be nourished by
spiritual food, which is the Word of God. You must take time
to fellowship with other believers. Your children need to have
Christian friends. You will find that your time in church is
time well spent.

Goals

Can you imagine a basketball game without set, predeter-
mined goals at each end of the playing floor toward which the
teams are constantly moving? What if a team's goal was not
there? Or what if it kept wandering around the gymnasium?
There would be a lot of dribbling, but not much of a game.

We need goals. Very little can be accomplished without
them. They give us a sense of direction and a purpose. We
need goals in our family life, in our spiritual life, and in our
business life.

Try to answer these questions:
- What do I want to have accomplished by the end of my
life? (Try writing your own obituary.)

• What do I want to have accomplished five years from now?

• What do I want to have accomplished by the end of the week?

• What do I want to have accomplished by the end of the day?

Once we know *where* we are going, we can then begin using our time more effectively to reach those goals.

When setting goals, make sure they are reasonably attainable. Setting a goal completely out of reach results in frustration. Know your limitations. Review the stages of your life. You can't tackle everything at every age. What you can't do when you are thirty may be fine when you are forty.

Take Inventory

It is an eye-opener to take inventory of the way time is spent. For a couple of days, keep a record of what you are doing. If you get up at 7:00 A.M., start then and continue through the day jotting down what you are doing each fifteen minutes. You will probably be surprised at the time you are wasting. Patrick J. Montana, time management specialist, says, "Studies show that almost everyone wastes two hours or more every day. That adds up when you think in terms of weeks, months and years. We spend 80 percent of our time on unimportant things that produce only 20 percent of the results."[3]

Take a hard look at *what* you are doing, both during and after office hours. Can you delete it? Delegate it? Defer it?

Are you involved in activities and organizations that are not really important to you? If so, you should consider dropping them. You *can't* do everything, so make your decisions based on your priorities and goals.

Calendars

The most important time-management tool is, of course, the calendar.

A master calendar should be used to *schedule* high-priority activities, not just used to keep track of the onslaught. Plan family time and time with God and write those times on the calendar. We need to give God and our human relationships at least as much respect as we do a dental appointment. Otherwise we will devote only *residual* time to them.

The master calendar is used to record appointments, meetings, games, practices—anything that can be scheduled. You may need two master calendars, one at home and one at work.

The Indispensable Notebook

To coordinate all activities and give you an ongoing "Things To Do" list, the notebook is an excellent organizational help. It is far more efficient than a pocket calendar because there is more room to write.

The notebook should be small enough to fit easily into any purse or pocket (about three by five inches). This notebook should go with you everywhere, and you can use it to make notations about all of your activities.

It is simple to put together. All that is needed is a binder, filler paper, and dividers with tabs. Those items are available at any office supply store.

The first section is the "calendar." Each page is for one day, and at the top put the day and date. Fill in the pages for about three months. Then enter all the appointments from the master calendar.

As things come up, jot down reminders to yourself on the appropriate day in the notebook "calendar." Both business and personal notations are made. If you need to call for an interview on next Tuesday, turn to next Tuesday and jot it down. Write down your menu-planning time and shopping time. When library books are checked out, write the number of books on the date they are due back. The more you use your notebook to take care of details, the less harried you will be. Once something is written down in the notebook, you can *forget* it.

As a day gets closer, more and more things are written on its page until the notations become a very effective "Things To Do" list. You may have on the list more things to do than you can possibly do in one day. Place them in order of priority, using the letters *A, B,* and *C.* The ones marked *A* must get done today; the ones marked *B* should get done today. The *C* items can wait until another day. Do the *A* things first. As each task gets done, cross it off. The things that don't get done are moved to another day. If anything is put off twice, make a decision: Is this *really* important? If not, out it goes. If so, the next day it's an *A.*

Your notebook will help you attain both long-range and short-range goals because you can use it to figure out what needs to be done, when it should be done, and how long it should take. Big projects can be broken down into segments that are more manageable.

Your notebook will have dividers with tabs, and you can use the other sections to fit your needs. You may want to use one section for "Notes," so you can write down ideas and information in business meetings. You may want a section for frequently used addresses and telephone numbers. You may want another section for meal planning and shopping lists.

Time on the Road

If you have to commute a long way to and from work, you may find that it would be worthwhile to move nearer your work or else to work nearer your home. Two or three hours of commuting time each day may be more than you should devote to travel. Some women, however, find commuting time useful. "My hour on the train in the morning gives me time to get ready for the day. Then on the way back home at night I can 'unwind' and change gears to adjust to being a mother again." Whatever your situation, you can use time on the road constructively. A cassette tape recorder is an excellent learning tool, and there are hundreds of motivational and inspirational tapes available to which you could listen while commuting. The address of a Christian tape library will be given at the end of this chapter.

Paper Moving

At work as at home, moving paper can get you bogged down and waste your time.

Stephanie Winston, expert on managing time and paperwork, says, "Whether you're the president of a corporation or in charge of your personal files, there are only three things you can do with a piece of paper. The first is to throw it out. The second is to do something with it, meaning a response of some kind—a letter or reply, a phone call, a visit. The third is to file it."[4]

The idea is to act quickly, making a decision about each piece of paper the first time you handle it. If you have a secretary, of course, much of this paperwork should be done for you, but you still may need to make some of the decisions.

Pitch it. Throw away routine memos and trivia. If you question whether you should keep it or not, it's probably something to throw out. *If in doubt, throw it out.* You'll never miss it.

Do it. If you *can* do it now, do it now. If it is something that needs to be done later, a letter to be answered or a phone call to be made, enter it on the appropriate day in your notebook. Put the paper in the folder marked "Things to Do."

File it. If it simply needs to be filed, put it in a file marked "To Be Filed."

To keep your "Things to Do" and "To Be Filed" files from getting overloaded, set aside a time on your calendar to take care of them.

Delegation

Delegation is the key to good leadership. Can someone else

do it better or faster or cheaper? Is someone else being paid to do what you are doing? Don't delegate what only you can do, but be honest about what can be more appropriately done by others. Are you afraid that someone else won't do the job as well as you? Are you afraid someone else will gain recognition? Are you afraid you can't teach someone else how to do the job properly?

Delegation benefits both you and your subordinates. You will have more time to concentrate on your leadership functions, and it gives your subordinates an opportunity to show their skills. Be sure to give credit to those who have worked on a project and praise them for a job well done.

Note: Mothers, your children are your subordinates. Delegate!

Decision Making

Much time is lost agonizing over decisions. Learn to make decisions as quickly as possible so that you can move on to other things. First of all, identify the problem. Write it down in one sentence. Then list the alternatives. Compare the alternatives and choose the best one. Then forget it. No one will make the right decision all the time; business leaders say if you are right half the time you are doing well.

Say No

No is a perfectly good word. Say it and stick with it. Decline requests that will not be in the best interest of your priorities and your goals. Rarely do we have to choose between right and wrong. It's usually between better and best. Don't take on any new involvement without asking yourself, "What can I drop to make time for this new thing?" That question will force you to review your priorities.

When people ask you to do something or take on a new project, don't give an answer right then. Tell them you need to think about it. Then think about it and pray about it and wait for the Lord's leading.

Finishing

The worst part about ironing is getting the ironing board set up, and the hardest thing about tackling any new project is getting started. But as important as starting is and as vital as progress is, your project will not count until it is *finished*. Do you start new projects with a burst of enthusiasm, then find them "blah" before the end of the week? Do you get overwhelmed by big projects?

The first thing to do to become a finisher is to know what you can handle. Don't take on jobs that are so huge you will be overwhelmed and soon defeated.

If you do have a big project to do, realistically assess the time it will take. Break it down into more manageable chunks. Learn to know your own attention span, and don't try to push yourself far beyond what is reasonable.

Learn to be a finisher. Discipline yourself to finish what you start. You will find it the greatest time-saver of all.

Notes

1 Edward R. Dayton and Ted W. Engstrom, *Strategy for Leadership* (Old Tappan, N.J.: Revell, 1979), p. 80.
2 Ted W. Engstrom, *The Making of a Christian Leader* (Grand Rapids: Zondervan, 1976), p. 101.
3 From "Ways to Stop Wasting Time on the Job," a copyrighted interview in *U.S. News & World Report*, 5 March 1979, p. 60.
4 From "How to Get Organized at Work and Home," a copyrighted interview in *U.S. News & World Report*, 7 May 1979, p. 76.

Suggested Reading

Edwin C. Bliss, *Getting Things Done* (New York: Bantam, 1976).
Edward R. Dayton and Ted W. Engstrom, *Strategy for Living* (Glendale, Calif.: Regal, 1976).
Charles E. Hummel, *Tyranny of the Urgent* (Downers Grove, Ill.: InterVarsity, 1974).
Anne Ortland, *Disciplines of the Beautiful Woman* (Waco, Tex.: Word, 1977).

Cassettes

Free loan library for cassette tapes (write for catalogue):
Christian Tape Library
13232 North Meridian Street
Carmel, Indiana 46032

Chapter Twelve

Choices

Many women today feel bombarded with alternatives, with choices that must be made. It can be dizzying.

Life was simpler, at least, when a woman was kept "pregnant in the winter and barefoot in the summer." She had fewer choices to make. No matter what anyone says, decision-making is tough.

All through life we have choices. Some of the decisions are little ones. It doesn't make much difference whether we have carrots or squash for dinner. But sometimes our choices make a vital change in the direction we are going in life.

Our choices are determined by our *values*. Values are what we *really* care about, not just what we say we believe. Our values are revealed by our choices, decisions, and actions.

Our biggest responsibility, however, is to be in the very center of God's will for our lives. He has a plan for each of us in the great mosaic of human history. So many people are afraid to allow God to lead because they think He will want them to suffer some terrible hardship or go off and live among the natives somewhere. God wants the very best for you. His plan is the perfect plan. By allowing Him to direct you, you will be able to experience the *abundant life*.

In order for you to know God's will in your life you must, first of all, belong to Him by accepting Jesus Christ as your Savior. Then you present yourself to Him as a *living sacrifice:*

> Therefore, I urge you, brothers, in view of God's mercy, to offer your bodies as living sacrifices, holy and pleasing to God—which is your spiritual worship. Do not conform any longer to the pattern of this world, but be transformed by the renewing of your mind. *Then you will be able to test and approve what God's will is—His good, pleasing and perfect will."*
>
> [Romans 12:1-2, NIV, emphasis mine]

If you place your whole life in the Lord's hands—your talents, your gifts, and even the desires of your heart—He will transform you by the renewing of your mind and make of your life the very best.

It is not necessary for us to worry about what God's will is: *"Commit* thy works unto the LORD, and thy *thoughts* shall be established (Proverbs 16:3, emphasis mine).

How to Know God's Will

The Written Word

The Bible remains the most practical Book for daily living ever written. It gives us the guidelines we need for making decisions. Our job is to know what it says, then abide by it.

One successful businessman I know reads from the book of Proverbs every morning before he goes to work. There are thirty-one chapters in Proverbs, so he reads one chapter each day of the month. He says that book gives him excellent guidance for his everyday business situations.

Some people have tried to use the Bible as a fortune-telling book—opening it at random, then blindly choosing a verse. That is not the way the Bible should be used. It is a reasonable book. It should be studied in a reasonable, systematic manner. If the Bible is new to you, get a good modern translation and start with the book of John.

Circumstances

God leads us, too, by the circumstances of life. Though He never intends for us to be "under the circumstances," that is, overwhelmed and confused by the happenings of life, He does use our circumstances in our decision-making processes.

Martha Evans, for example, was catapulted into the world of business by a tragedy that struck her home.

"I had never really planned on working," she says simply. "I went to college for a year in the nineteen fifties and majored in 'animal husbandry' to get my 'Mrs.' degree. We joked about it then, but all my friends felt the same way. We weren't interested in careers.

"My husband, Jack, had a heart attack and died when he was forty years old. We had one boy in high school, a girl in junior high, and another boy in fifth grade.

"By the time we paid all the bills and taxes and everything, there wasn't much left of the insurance money. I began to see that I needed to think about my future. A whole chunk of my life was gone. It wasn't healthy for me to latch on to the kids so totally for emotional support. I began praying about it, and God showed me that it would be good for the children and for me if I could work. It surprised me at first, because I'd always been so outspoken against working mothers! But it's been the best thing I could have done. Getting busy and getting involved with other people has helped me to come to terms with my own loss, and I'm less tempted to feel sorry for myself."

Competent Counsel

Many times it is important to seek the wisdom of a mature Christian, one who can see the spiritual implications of any decision. God tells us to walk not "in the counsel of the ungodly" (Psalm 1:1). A spiritually mature person can often see potential problems and pitfalls and give you counsel undergirded by truth.

Sometimes it is necessary to go outside the Christian community for counsel. It is usually well worth the expense to seek the best possible medical, legal, or financial advice when making a decision in any of those areas.

If you are married, your husband needs to be actively involved in your decisions. That idea ignites fury among some people, but it is, nevertheless, true. If you want to be in God's will, you must follow His order for families and follow your husband's leadership. You cannot be in God's will if you are refusing your husband's leadership in your home.

One woman, for example, was leading a Bible study on the marriage relationship. It happened that she was working outside the home and had been working since before her children were born. The book they were using as a study guide stated in no uncertain terms that a wife should *not* work outside the home.

"When I saw what the book said, I became very upset," she says. "I was so afraid that I was out of God's will, doing something really wrong, even though I had prayed about it and had my husband's full approval and support.

"I went to him and showed him what the book said. He said to me, 'Honey, you know we both went before God with that decision. He opened the door to a job for you that fits in perfectly with our family life. I am proud of your abilities, and I know that our children are not being hurt. You made the decision to work under my authority. There are too many things involved for anyone to dictate to another person whether it's right or wrong for her to have a job.' I realized once again how very important it is for a woman to look to her husband for guidance."

Inner Peace

It is dangerous, indeed, to make decisions based only on feelings. But God does use our feelings in the decision-making process.

If we have uneasiness about a certain course of action, we had better reconsider it. When in Doubt, Don't is not a bad slogan to keep in mind. In the business world, those feelings are called "red flags," warnings of potential trouble. Pay attention to the "red flags."

After you have gone to the Word, analyzed the circumstances, prayed for God's guidance, and sought counsel, then you will probably have an inner peace about the decision. I repeat, however, that we can't go on feelings alone, because our emotions can play tricks on us. But they have an important role in the decision-making process.

Answered Prayer

With regard to finding a job, changing jobs, or making a decision to stop working, many things must be considered. Every woman must go to God with those decisions and earnestly seek His perfect will for her life.

Judith Reynolds found that God answers prayer and provides specific direction if we will trust Him to lead us. Judith and her husband live in a beautiful home with extra rooms. They decided that God had provided the home for them, so they would honor Him by converting the extra rooms into a missionary apartment. The only problem was that there was no money available at the time to do the work involved. Within a few days of their decision they heard about a missionary family needing a place to live. At the time, Judith's children were all in school, and she had just been elected president of her local Christian Women's Club, which had a monthly luncheon.

"I just went before the Lord and asked Him to work out all the problems and complications. I had done some substitute teaching, but that was very unpredictable, so I didn't think that was the answer. If I were to go to work, I knew that I would have to be free to fulfill my responsibility to Christian Women's Club, and I would have to be home when the children got home from school. I just prayed that the Lord would show me what He wanted me to do.

"Within fifteen minutes of my praying, the telephone rang. It was the principal of the local junior high school. The music teacher had quit suddenly, and could I finish out the year for her? It would be a half-time position, and I would work only in the mornings. He even told me I could leave early once in a while if I needed to, which was exactly what was required on the days of the monthly luncheons. It was a direct, unquestionable answer to prayer.

"We finished the missionary apartment, but the Lord has not led me to leave my teaching position. He might someday, but He hasn't yet. I do enjoy the creative aspects of the work, and I believe God is using me in the public school system to minister to kids who may know no other Christian."

Time Is Right?

If you believe the time is right for you to become a wage earner or you believe that someday you will need to enter the labor force, here is some help.

The first thing you need to do is to assess your abilities, training, and experience. Even if you have never held a paying job, you have much to offer a prospective employer. Look at yourself honestly. If you have been home with children for several years, you have been working in many capacities: teacher, chauffeur, buyer, accountant, manager, chef, janitor, nurse, and many others. You are *not* inept.

In fact, many employers see you as a very competent, mature individual and may be looking for someone just like you. In *The Working Mother's Complete Handbook*, Gloria Norris and JoAnn Miller quote Felice Schwartz, president of Catalyst, an organization dedicated to finding jobs for women in mid-life, who tells of one: managing a McDonald's restaurant. "McDonald's does *not* want someone just out of college," explains Schwartz. "They want a thirty-five-year-old woman who has the authority and presence to manage the average McDonald's staff of sixty-five kids. Someone who appreciates a good career opportunity, but doesn't mind the tough work."[1]

Many women suffer from one of two basic problems when assessing their own abilities.

• They have a poor self-image, the tendency to put themselves down, and the totally unwarranted feeling of being inferior to others. These women seem to suffer most of all from tunnel vision. They see themselves destined to remain forever on the lowest rung of the ladder. These women are the ones most likely to be bored in the homemaking role or apathetic on the job. Their lives are limited by "impossibility thinking."

• The second kind of problem is a tendency to unrealistic expectations. One woman who married right out of high school has been dabbling for several years in different hobbies, trying to turn them into profit-making ventures. At one time she was making macrame plant hangers by the scores, then she became interested in quilting and embroidering. For a while she sold cosmetics, then she tried her hand at writing poetry.

Now she says, "What I'd really like to do is manage a small firm. No, I don't want to take any business courses—that would be such a bore. I'd just like to have my own little operation that I could manage. That sounds like fun."

The woman is suffering from unrealistic expectations. What she must do is come to grips with what she *really* wants to do, what her actual talents are, and what she can hope to accomplish. If managing a small firm is what she wants to do, she will have to either own the firm (which takes determination, courage, and *money*) or gain enough experience in the business world so that someone else would entrust her with the responsibility.

Plan Ahead

A more reasonable strategy for the woman staying home with children for a number of years is to *use* those years to prepare for that future day when she will want or need to find employment. The reason we have had the phenomenon of the "displaced homemaker" is that women have not considered their *life stages*. Women now can anticipate living about eighty years. It is not necessary to do *everything* at every age. It is quite possible to stay home with the children for several years and go to school or work part time for several more years, all the time preparing for the day when the nest will be empty or at least inhabited by *big* birds!

Too many women must find a job, *any* job, in the midst of an emotional and/or economic crisis. Those women usually find the adjustment into the working world a hard one, and many feel bitter about it.

If a woman can prepare and plan during those years at home, she might even enjoy her full-time motherhood years more. That is a good time to develop skills or get more education. Planning and preparing will give her an outlet and something to occupy her mind while doing her more mundane chores.

Women who are considering going to work because they feel their lives are not full enough might think about expanding their work for the Lord instead. Though each of us should be involved in the Lord's work to some extent, there is no doubt that a person can devote more time to ministry if he or she is not working at another demanding job.

A woman named Ellen has been a highly paid, competent secretary for twenty years. Her children are now in high school. She and her husband recently decided that they would adjust their standard of living so that she could quit her job.

"My basic reason for leaving my job," she said, "is that the Lord has been leading me to greater involvement in the ministry of neighborhood Bible studies. I became very aware of the fact that I can't do everything. We are excited about what the Lord has in store for us."

Not everyone, of course, has the option of not working, but each person does need to be sensitive to the Lord's leading.

The Lord may want you in a secular job because of the tremendous opportunities for establishing friendships with people there who need to know the Lord. You can be a powerful witness to the people at your place of work and have a ministry that will change lives.

Build Your Confidence

Whatever a person does in life, it's important to be self-confident. Why do most of us lack confidence in ourselves? We are afraid of people, afraid of criticism, or afraid someone won't like us.

The Bible tells us that real confidence comes from God: "Fear of man will prove to be a snare, but whoever trusts in the Lord is kept safe" (Proverbs 29:25, NIV).

I believe that God would have us develop this confidence by many different means. Speaking before groups of people is an excellent way to become more confident in all areas. Accept every opportunity you have to speak publicly. Giving programs, teaching Sunday school, or being chairman of a committee will help develop confidence.

Courses are available that are especially designed to help people develop confidence and lose their fear of others. Some are led by trained instructors for a stated number of weeks. In other cases, groups meet once a week or twice a month, and the members of the group rotate the responsibilities of speaking and evaluating. Whichever approach you prefer, you will find wide ranges in age, education, and interests.

Working Part Time

For many women, the best answer to the question of working is a part-time job. They generally consider taking care of the family needs their primary role, but they like having part-time work. In that way they can make a little money and stay involved in their fields without the stress at home that often comes when a mother works full time. As Hoffman and Nye say, "One role (homemaker) may not be enough, but two (homemaker and full-time employee) are too many."[2]

Kay Lumber, a woman who now works full time at a large metropolitan bank, and whose career is advancing rapidly, says she believes her career was not hurt by what she laughingly calls a "seven-year maternity leave."

"I worked as a teller for two years before our babies were born," she says. "I wanted very much to stay home with the children. Maybe I realized more than most women the privilege of caring for your babies, because we lost two of our children. Even in my grief I was determined to really enjoy our two girls. You couldn't have dragged me away from them. As they grew older, though, and got in school, I did some part-time work for various firms before I went back to the bank. I worked 'mother's hours' at the bank for about nine years, until the girls were old enough to stay by themselves. Then I had the opportunity to go to work full time with the promise of advancement. The time seemed to be right for the family. My husband is very supportive of what I do and spends a great deal of time with the girls."

In that case, part-time work seemed to be an ideal solution, leading to a full-time career once the children were older.

Others Frustrated

Other women have reported that attempting a part-time career didn't work so well for them. Linda Hendrix McPharlin reports her search for a good part-time job: "A part-time job would have helped tremendously. But after six months of searching I learned that most employers will not believe for a minute that anything worthwhile can be contributed by a part-time worker. Only a year and a half earlier I had earned

$1,000 a month at a responsible administrative job. Now I was worth $1.65 an hour and good for nothing more than telephone soliciting."[3] Though there seem to be some indications of change, many women experience the same frustration. Part-time work, in general, is not highly respected or rewarded. The pay is often so low that expenses may exceed earnings. And the part-time employee generally is not given the benefits (vacation time, sick days, medical and health insurance, and pension plan, to name a few) that are usually available to full-time workers. Many times a mother will accept the lower pay of a part-time job so that she can stay active in her field during the years that her children are young. Though it is not the answer for everyone, part-time work makes sense for many mothers.

Working at Home

Another arrangement that many women have found effective is running a business at home. One woman with a baby is an accountant and keeps the books for several firms in her home. Another woman has a typing service. Other women work on craft projects that are sold through local boutiques, or develop businesses based on homemaking skills such as cleaning, catering, or sewing. Many women who choose to stay home with children are earning extra money by babysitting for other mothers. One woman even started a business called The Surrogate Wife. What she does for her clients is run errands that wives used to run, before they went to work. She operates car pools, takes care of the dry cleaning, gets shoes repaired, cares for Christmas shopping, and does other such jobs. She has built up a profitable business.

Certainly there are advantages to working out of your home. It is convenient, many times you don't need to pay a babysitter, the quarters are "free" in the sense that there is no need to pay rent, and the schedule can be worked around other activities.

The disadvantages are numerous, however, and any woman thinking of setting up a business at home should consider them carefully.

• Will it be worthwhile economically? Will your income be more than your expenses?

• Do you have the self-discipline for it? You will have to force yourself to work on a schedule. Women who work in an office don't think much about the mess at home while they are away from it. But the woman who works at home can easily be distracted by children and/or housework. It helps to establish "work hours" that are honored. Otherwise, projects simply will not be completed.

• Can you cope with interruptions? If your work requires concentration, interruptions can be a big problem. Decide when your "working hours" are, and stick to them. Tell your friends not to phone or come to visit during those hours. If you love to visit with friends, you will find that especially hard, but it is necessary. If you don't get "tough" with yourself, your business will remain a hobby forever.

If you do start a business at home, be sure you charge enough to cover your expenses and to give you a profit. You can't stay in business long if your expenses are more than your earnings.

Direct Sales

Another area of opportunity for women who prefer to work at a job that can give them flexible scheduling is direct sales. All kinds of items can be sold through direct sales, from vacuum cleaners to household furnishings. Many different methods are employed, from door-to-door sales to the home party system. Sometimes the person simply works for commissions from the sale of the products; other times she brings other people into the business as well.

One Woman's Story

Here is the story of how one woman allowed God to help

her make a big decision.

Virginia is a legal secretary and has two daughters in elementary school. She had worked full time since before she was married, except for a couple of brief stays at home when the girls were born.

"Don had never objected to my working. As a matter of fact, he was proud of my abilities. When the girls entered elementary school, I was working full time for one of the judges in the court of appeals.

"Don and I talked at length about whether I should continue working full time. I wanted to find a job where I could work in my field but only certain hours, so I could leave after the girls left for school and be home before they got home.

"So we began praying that something meeting those requirements would open up.

"Unknown to me, a Jewish lawyer in a nearby part of the city had just set up practice with a partner. They were just getting started and had only so much money a week they felt they could pay a secretary. They couldn't afford a full-time secretary.

"Don and I had set up some very specific criteria. I thought I should get a certain amount per hour. I could work from 8:30 A.M. to 2:30 P.M. I was teaching a Bible study on Wednesdays, so we prayed that I'd be able to have Wednesdays off. We also only had one car, so we prayed that I could make enough so that we could get another car.

"I began reading ads in newspapers and calling. I called one that was for statistical typing and thought, 'That sounds pretty tedious, but I'll check it out.' I made an appointment with them for an interview.

"I made another call, and they put me on 'hold.' While I was sitting there on 'hold,' all of a sudden one of the ads sort of leaped off the paper at me. I hadn't seen it before. It said 'Part-time legal secretary' and gave the address and telephone number. It was not far from my house.

'I just hung up on the person who had me on 'hold' and dialed the number. I made an appointment for an interview the next day.

"When I went in, I met the Jewish lawyer I mentioned before.

"He tells me, now, that he didn't like me very much because I was so definite about what I could and couldn't do, but he calculated the number of hours. It was *exactly* what they had decided they could afford, so I got the job. He agreed to the hours I needed, and I even got Wednesdays off."

The most exciting part of this woman's story is that the Jewish attorney became very interested in spiritual matters.

"In the work situation," says Virginia, "I had a policy of always allowing the other person to be the one to bring up spiritual matters. I would just follow the other person's lead. In business it just seems to be the best policy. But, anyway, it was so great—Scott brought up spiritual matters constantly, almost every day! We got into some terrific discussions about Moses and Abraham."

Eventually that Jewish attorney received Jesus Christ as the Messiah.

As God was guiding Virginia's choices, it was not luck or chance that caused those events to take place. They all were part of the great design of which God Himself was the artist.

Notes

[1] Gloria Norris and JoAnn Miller, *The Working Mother's Complete Handbook* (New York: Dutton, 1979), p. 196.
[2] Lois Wladis Hoffman and F. Ivan Nye, *Working Mothers* (San Francisco: Jossey-Bass, 1974), p. 57.
[3] Linda Hendrix McPharlin, "Do I Have the Right to Be a Working Mother?" *Redbook*, August 1976, p. 42. Used by permission.

Suggested Reading

Ted W. Engstrom, *The Making of a Christian Leader* (Grand Rapids: Zondervan, 1976).
Zig Ziglar, *See You at the Top* (Gretna, La.: Pelican, 1978).

Chapter Thirteen

Beyond Success

Jo Ellen was born on a cold wintry night in a small coal-mining town in the hills of West Virginia. The wind howled through the cracks in the crudely-built house that Jo Ellen would remember as "home."

"I was just a little girl when Papa left home," Jo Ellen says. "He left Mama with five kids to raise, and no one but the Lord to lean on. Those were hard years. We were on welfare, and I hated that snooty welfare lady who came to our house. I hated her blond hair and that pink suit that she wore. She never would sit back all the way in our chairs. I think she was afraid of getting poor people's germs.

"Mama took in ironing from the rich folks who lived on the other side of town. I'd watch them drive up to our rickety house in their big fancy cars, and I hated them, too.

"It drove me crazy when I'd come home from school. There would be Mama, standing over her ironing board, singing about Jesus. What had Jesus ever done for her?

"Mama taught me that I had to just accept my lot in life. 'Poor folks,' she would say, 'have to get along in a rich man's world. Just accept it, honey.'

"Mama was wonderful to us kids. We knew that she loved us totally. She wanted to protect us from getting hurt, so she

taught us that we should know our place in life and stay there.
'Don't rock the boat, honey,' she used to say, laughing. 'You'll
only get wet.'

"Somehow I became a very determined young woman. I
was determined, first of all, that I wouldn't be left in a position where I'd have to go on welfare and take in ironing. I was
determined that the rich kids wouldn't look down their noses
at my kids.

"I didn't know how I was going to do it, but I didn't want my
kids to ever feel inferior because of where they lived or the
clothes they wore.

By the time Jo Ellen was eighteen, she had heard that there
were jobs in the city, good jobs. When she climbed aboard
that big Greyhound bus, she vowed she would never return to
the town with the rickety house. She found work with a
pharmaceutical company, and soon she was making enough
money for her needs with some left over each month to send
home to Mama.

"Most of the girls like me," said Jo Ellen, "were perfectly
happy to work on the line and get overtime once in a while.
Somehow I couldn't be satisfied with that. I felt that there was
opportunity for me, and I wasn't willing to accept that the
lowest-paying job had to be my lot in life. Why couldn't I
become a supervisor?"

Jo Ellen's company, like many others during that time, was
looking for women to promote, and she was determined to be
promoted. When it finally happened, she felt rather smug.
She almost enjoyed the animosity that came from the women
who were envious and the men who were resentful. But Jo
Ellen didn't care. She grabbed the opportunity with a ven-
geance, resolved to show everyone, especially Mama and that
God of hers, that she could make it on her own.

"Mama thought that being poor was our cross to bear,
and I resented her God who let us be cold and hungry when I
was a little girl. I thought He must be a terrible God to treat

people that way. I wanted no part of God or religion."

Shortly after her first promotion, Jo Ellen met Mac, a man who worked at another manufacturing firm. They married, moved into a bigger apartment, and began to enjoy living on their combined incomes.

"Then I got pregnant," says Jo Ellen. "I worked until the week Jeremy was born, but I was determined to go back. Those first few months were hard because I was so tired all the time. He was a colicky baby, and my sitters kept quitting on me. Then the second child came along, and I went through a terrible time trying to find a sitter. I remember one sitter especially. When I went to pick up the kids, I'd notice that Jeremy had black eyes and bruises. She kept telling me that he fell, but finally I realized that *she* was doing it. They never went back there!"

Jo Ellen nearly collapsed with exhaustion, and Mac showed the strain. He helped her with the housework and gave the children their baths at night, but there was just too much to do. The second baby began having ear infections, and that was the last straw. Jo Ellen quit her job.

"While I was home, I kept remembering Mama, and how she was always home, always available to us kids. I wanted to be that kind of mother. It surprised me that I enjoyed being home so much.

"The only problem was money—the lack of it. We had become accustomed to living on both of our incomes, and we just weren't making it. Mac started moonlighting, working at odd jobs, working sixteen hours a day.

"When I saw the pressure that Mac was under, trying to support all of us on the small amount of money he was able to make, I got scared. I had nightmares. In my dreams I saw Papa, frustrated and miserable, trying to feed our big family. That was why he left, of course. He just couldn't do it."

Jo Ellen became resentful of the babies and Mac, dwelling on how much money she would be making by now if she hadn't had to quit. She couldn't understand herself. One minute she would be happy, enjoying her children, and the next moment she would feel like she was in a cage, scratching and clawing, hysterically wanting *out*.

"I became bitter toward Mac because he couldn't provide better for me. If there was ever anything I wanted it was to live in a nice place. We had to move back into a dumpy apartment when I quit work, and I hated it. I hated the dingy walls and the beat-up furniture.

"I kept thinking about Mama. She lived her whole life in a place far worse than that one. I never once heard her complain. She always had a smile on her face and something positive to say. What was it that had given Mama a peaceful heart in the midst of such hardship?"

Jo Ellen decided that Mama must have been a fool to have settled for such misery. She made up her mind that she was going to get out of that miserable apartment if it was the last thing she ever did. She got a job with her old company once more.

Jo Ellen was determined to be a success, which to her meant a nice house, a nice car, and nice clothes. She told her boss that she wanted to be advanced and that she was willing to work hard and long to show that she could get the job done.

Jo Ellen threw herself into her work. When she got home, she was too tired to enjoy her children or her husband. At times they seemed to be in a different world. She felt she was losing touch with them, but she was too preoccupied to care much. A promotion was opening up at the company, and all she could think about was getting that promotion.

When she didn't get the promotion, she sank into a deep depression. Mac tried to cheer her up, but she felt as though he were a stranger. He meant nothing to her. They had nothing in common anymore.

She kept working diligently, and eventually she got an even better promotion. Her pay increased dramatically. She and Mac bought a nice house in a lovely neighborhood, but Jo Ellen wasn't satisfied. It was all right, but not *that* great. The new car she had wanted so badly soon was dented and no longer seemed so splendid.

Jo Ellen felt overwhelmed by frustration. She had achieved more than she had ever thought was possible, yet she wasn't happy. She had a house that she would have considered a palace when she was a child, yet she was miserable. She felt that her marriage was doomed and that she didn't even know her children. What was life all about, anyway?

Then one day Jo Ellen's brother called to tell her that Mama was really sick. She was in the hospital and might not make it through the night. Jo Ellen got the next flight out of town, and when she arrived at the hospital, all of her brothers and sisters were there.

"Mama's been asking for you," said a sister softly.

Jo Ellen quietly entered the hospital room and was shocked to see Mama so thin, so *thin*.

"Oh, Mama," Jo Ellen whispered.

"Hush, now, honey," Mama said. "I want to say something to you and there's not much time. I want you to have this."

She held out to Jo Ellen her old, worn, and tattered Bible. The pages were yellowed. But it was so much a part of Mama's life that Jo Ellen didn't want to take it.

Jo Ellen took Mama's hand. "I wish I could believe it, Mama," she said. "I really do. But I don't understand what difference it makes. You loved God all those years, but you had *nothing*."

"Oh, honey, you are wrong about that. Maybe I didn't have what the world calls success, but I had everything that was really important. This Book tells us that the truth shall make us *free*."

"Free from *what*?"

"Knowing God sets us free from a lot of things—our bondage to sin and guilt, of course. But it also sets us free from

the misery of selfishness and sets us free from having to depend on our circumstances for happiness. It's not wrong to
work hard and do well. God often blesses people in that way.
But when you really *trust* Him, you see, you begin to realize
that those things are not so important. We're just passing
through this life, honey. We may get some hard knocks along
the way. But we can know, through it all, that God loves us."

She held up her Bible again.

"This Book will tell you about a Friend of mine," Mama said
softly. "You've heard about Him all your life, but you were
always too angry to get to know Him. He wants to be your
Friend, too."

Jo Ellen sat in the darkened room with Mama. Suddenly all
her success in the business world paled in importance.

Mama was talking. "You know, honey, I want to give you
this Book as a gift. I can lay it here on the table for you, but
unless you reach out and *take* it, it won't really belong to you.
That's just like God's gift to us. He gave us Jesus so we would
never be separated from Him throughout all eternity. Jesus is
God's gift to us. But unless you reach out and accept that gift,
it isn't really yours."

Jo Ellen realized that Mama was giving her something far
more precious than money or success, and she sobbed uncon-
trollably.

Then she heard the gentlest, sweetest voice in all the world
singing softly. The haunting melody took Jo Ellen back to the
times when Mama would hold her closely in the rocker and
sing her to sleep.

As she listened to Mama sing her last lullaby, Jo Ellen felt
the wall of resistance crumbling. She knew that she had built
that wall between herself and God. Suddenly, she realized
that God *loved* her. He had loved her all along.

The Savior is waiting to enter your heart,
Why don't you let Him come in?

There's nothing in this world to keep you apart,
What is your answer to Him?

Time after time He has waited before,
And now He is waiting again
To see if you're willing to open the door,
O, how He wants to come in.

If you'll take one step t'ward the Savior, my friend,
You'll find His arms open wide;
Receive Him, and all of your darkness will end,
Within your heart He'll abide.

Time after time He has waited before,
And now He is waiting again
To see if you're willing to open the door,
O, how He wants to come in.

*Ralph Carmichael**

APPENDIX

Quick Recipes for Busy Families

Perfect Chili

Brown:
    1½ pounds ground beef
    1 onion, chopped
    1 green pepper, chopped

Drain off grease and add:
    1 large can Brooks hot chili beans
    1 large can tomato juice
    1 or 2 tablespoons chili powder
    2 teaspoons sugar

Cover and simmer 1 hour or longer. Makes six *hearty* servings.
Double recipe and freeze half for another day.
Serve with cooked macaroni if you like.

Quick Main Dishes

Green peppers stuffed with canned corn beef hash.

Porcupine meat balls made with hamburger, tomato soup, and Minute rice.

Hot dogs, slit, and cheese strips stuffed into slits. Wrap with bacon; secure with toothpicks. Broil, slit side down. Turn, and broil until bacon is done.

Hurry-Up Supper

Melt in frying pan:
    1 tablespoon margarine

Add:
    1 6-oz. can pink salmon (drain; remove bones if desired)

Add:
    6 unbeaten eggs and scramble together

Serve with tomato soup and hot rolls. Serves four or five.

Hamburger Noodle Casserole

Brown in large skillet:
    1½ lbs. hamburger
    1 chopped onion

Drain off excess grease. Meanwhile cook 8 oz. noodles according
to package directions. Drain. Add to the meat mixture:
    drained noodles
    1 can undiluted tomato soup
    1 8-oz. tomato sauce

Add:
    1 c. Velveeta cheese chunks

Stir and simmer a few minutes until cheese melts. *Optional—*
add can of drained corn. Makes six large servings. (Casserole can
be frozen.)

                                                        Sue Runyan

Sally's Mom's Egg Foo Yong (Keep ingredients for this dish on hand
for emergencies.)

Beat slightly:
    6 eggs

Add:
    ¼ c. chopped onion
    ¼ c. chopped green pepper
    1 7-oz. can tuna, well drained

1 can drained Chinese vegetables (save liquid)
1 teaspoon Accent
1 teaspoon soy sauce
½ teaspoon salt

Blend gently with fork. Make patties using ⅓ cup of mixture for each. Fry in hot oil. Flatten slightly, shaping cake by pushing edges with turner. Brown one side, then the other, adding oil to pan as necessary. Serve hot with rice and soy gravy. Makes six to eight patties.

Soy Gravy

Heat to boiling:
   ¾ c. liquid from Chinese vegetables
   ¼ c. water
   1 tablespoon cornstarch
   1 teaspoon sugar
   2 tablespoons soy sauce

Blend and thicken. Serve over egg foo yong patties.

Chow Mein

Brown 1½ lbs. hamburger and drain off fat.

Add:
   2 c. water
   2 c. diced celery
   ½ c. diced onions
   1 teaspoon salt

Simmer until vegetables are tender. Thicken with:
   1 heaping tablespoon cornstarch
   ½ c. water

Add:
   2 c. drained bean sprouts
   1 tablespoon soy sauce

Cover; simmer till heated through. Serve over chow mein noodles. Makes six to eight servings.

Sonja Jones

Tuna Noodle Bake

Cook and drain 4 oz. noodles.

Drain and flake 1 6½-oz. can tuna.

Heat together:
  1 c. pasteurized process cheese spread
  1 can cream mushroom soup
  ½ c. milk

Toss together noodles, tuna, and sauce. Place in 2-quart casserole; top with bread crumbs, crumbled potato chips, or paprika, if desired. *Optional:* Add 1 c. cooked and drained peas and/or 2 chopped hard-cooked eggs to mixture. Bake at 350° until hot and bubbly. Makes four or five servings.

Ever-ready Meat Loaf

Press 4 slices of bread in small bowl. Pour on milk to cover.
  Soak for a few minutes. Mix with:
2½ lbs. lean ground beef
½ lb. sausage
3 eggs, beaten
1 large chopped onion
¼ c. chopped green pepper
½ cup chili sauce or catsup
salt and pepper
½ teaspoon garlic powder

Mix thoroughly. Divide into loaves the right size for your family and freeze individually. When ready to use, thaw or put right from freezer into baking pan. Top with 2 carrots, cut into sticks. If thawed, bake about 1 hour at 375°. *Drain off grease.* Top loaf with 1 or 2 1-lb. cans tomato-pepper-onion combination. Add more green pepper, if you like.
Bake another 30 minutes or so.
Can be baked in microwave or conventional oven. Each recipe makes three meat loaves that will *each* serve four or five persons.

Estella Copple

Baked Haddock

Thaw frozen fish. (A 1-lb. package serves three.) Soak fish in milk about 10 minutes, then drain. Cut in big squares. Sprinkle on about ¼ teaspoon salt and ¼ teaspoon lemon-pepper seasoning. Place in buttered baking dish. Place 1 tablespoon grated or chopped onion on top of each piece. Squeeze lemon on top liberally.

Bake at 375° about 40 minutes, or in microwave about 10 minutes.

Estella Copple

Goop

Combine in Crock-Pot:
    1 pkg. beef stew meat
    1 large can tomato soup (do not dilute)
    1 pkg. dry onion soup mix

Cook on low all day (needs at least 7 or 8 hours). Serve over rice. Kids love it! Serves four or five.

Easy Chicken Casserole

    2 5-oz. cans Swanson's boned chicken
    1 small can evaporated milk
    1 small can Chinese noodles
    1 can cream of chicken soup
    1 can condensed chicken with rice soup

Place mixture in casserole; top with crumbled potato chips if desired. Bake at 350° for 1 hour or until bubbly. Serves four.

Sandy Ray

Salmon Patties

Mix and shape into patties:
    1 large can salmon
    ½ c. cracker crumbs

1 or 2 eggs
¼ teaspoon salt
⅛ teaspoon pepper
Fry in oil until brown. Serves four.

Marge Spolyar

Super Subs

Cut in half mini-loaves of French bread (one per person). Arrange assorted lunch meat, sliced tomatoes, green peppers, onion, olives. Use your imagination! Top with Swiss cheese. Broil until cheese melts and sandwich is hot.

For pizza subs, top mini-loaves of French bread, cut in half, with hamburger (browned with onion, then drained). Spoon over canned spaghetti sauce. Top with Mozzarella cheese, grated or sliced very thin.

Rosalie Alexander

Ham Sandwiches (These are *great* to have on hand!)

Mix together:
   1 stick butter, softened
   3 tablespoons mustard
   1½ tablespoons poppy seeds
   1 teaspoon Worcestershire sauce
   1 medium onion, grated

For 16 sandwiches, you will need 3 lb. sliced ham, 1 lb. sliced Swiss cheese, and 16 hamburger buns. Spread mixture on buns, then add ham and cheese. Heat in moderate oven until cheese melts and sandwiches are hot.

Wrap each sandwich in foil if they are to be frozen. *Thaw before heating.* Leave in foil to heat in conventional oven; take out and wrap in paper towel to heat in microwave. Makes 16 sandwiches.

Sandy Ray

Tuna Burgers

Combine:

1 6½-oz. can drained tuna
2 tablespoons chopped onion
2 tablespoons chopped pickle relish
½ cup mayonnaise or salad dressing
salt and pepper

Spread on toasted English muffin halves, sprinkle with shredded Cheddar cheese. Broil until hot and bubbly. Serves four.

Mini Pizza (Mini Pizza and Pigs-in-a-Blanket are main dishes or hearty snacks kids can fix. An adult should be nearby unless children are old enough to use stove alone.)

English muffins, split and toasted
Spread with prepared spaghetti sauce.
Sprinkle with Mozzarella cheese.
Broil or microwave until cheese melts.

Pigs-in-a-Blanket

For each person:

1 refrigerator biscuit
1 hot dog

Preheat oven to 450°. With a rolling pin, flatten biscuit to ¼" between 2 pieces of waxed paper. Peel away waxed paper and wrap hot dogs in dough. Seal by pinching dough with fingers. Place on well-greased cookie sheet. Bake 15 minutes.

Broccoli Even a Kid Could Love

Use rolling pin to crumb:
½ lb. Ritz crackers

Melt and add to crackers:
½ stick margarine

Melt over low heat:
1 lb. Velveeta cheese

Add to cheese:
½ stick margarine

Prepare 2 small packages of frozen chopped broccoli. Drain. Stir broccoli into cheese mixture. Layer half the crumbs, all the broccoli and cheese, and the remaining crumbs. Bake 15 minutes at 350°. (If you make ahead and refrigerate, bake 30 minutes.)

Joyce Runyan

Easy Cherry Delight

Place 1 can cherry pie filling in greased pan. Sprinkle 1 yellow cake mix right from box onto filling. Pour 1 stick melted butter evenly over cake mix. Bake at 350° for 30 minutes. Eat plain or top with ice cream or whipped cream.

Easy Peach Cobbler

Melt 2 sticks butter or margarine in oblong baking dish.

Combine:
2 c. sugar
2 c. flour
4 teaspoons baking powder
1½ c. milk

Pour mixture over melted butter. Top with one large can freestone peaches with juice. *Do not stir or mix.* Sprinkle with sugar and a little nutmeg. Bake at 375° for 1 hour. Serve hot with ice cream. Makes ten to twelve servings.

Carol Pearman

Seven-Layer Cookies

Melt 1 stick butter in oblong baking dish.

Add in layers:
    1 c. graham cracker crumbs
    1 small can coconut
    1 small package chocolate chips
    1 c. condensed milk (not evaporated)
    1 c. chopped pecans

Bake at 350° for 30-40 minutes. Cut in squares.

Six-Week Muffins (Do you like to have hot bread but hate the hassle?)

Combine:
    10-oz. box raisin bran
    3 c. sugar
    5 c. flour
    5 teaspoons soda
    2 teaspoons salt

Add:
    4 beaten eggs
    1 c. melted Crisco
    1 quart buttermilk

Mix and store in covered bowl in refrigerator up to six weeks. Fill greased muffin tins or paper liners three-fourths full. Bake at 375° for 15 to 20 minutes.

Goodies

Bring to boil 1 cup light corn syrup and 1 cup sugar. Remove from heat.
Mix in 1 cup peanut butter.
Add 6 cups Rice Krispies.
Press into *buttered* 9″ x 13″ pan.

Melt together:
    6-oz. pkg. semisweet chocolate chips
    6-oz. pkg. butterscotch chips

Spread on top.

Martha Perry

Quick Chocolate Fudge

Put unmixed into bowl:
    1 lb. box powdered sugar
    ½ cup cocoa
    1 stick butter
    ¼ cup milk
    ½ cup nuts

Put in microwave oven for 2 minutes. Stir well. Add 1 tablespoon vanilla. Pour into a greased 8″ x 8″ square dish. Freeze 20 minutes or refrigerate 1 hour. For peanut butter fudge, use ½ cup peanut butter instead of cocoa. For chocolate-peanut butter fudge, add 1 tablespoon peanut butter to original recipe.

Sue Moster

246   3464

Moster, Mary Beth

When mom goes to work.

Date Due

MAR. 1 5 1981			
MAY 3 1 1981			
MAY 3 1 1987			
OCT 1 1 1987			

BRODART, INC. Cat. No. 23 233 Printed in U.S.A.